THE

INSURANCE
MAZE

How You Can **Save Money**

on Insurance—and Still Get the

Coverage You Need

KIMBERLY LANKFORD

Columnist, *Kiplinger's Personal Finance*

KAPLAN) PUBLISHING

This publication is designed to provide accurate and authoritative information in regard to the subject matter covered. It is sold with the understanding that the publisher is not engaged in rendering legal, accounting, or other professional service. If legal advice or other expert assistance is required, the services of a competent professional person should be sought.

President, Kaplan Publishing: Roy Lipner
Vice President and Publisher: Maureen McMahon
Development Editor: Trey Thoelcke
Production Editor: Leah Strauss
Typesetter: Caitlin Ostrow
Cover Designer: Michael Warrell, Design Solutions

© 2006 by Kimberly Lankford

Published by Kaplan Publishing,
a division of Kaplan, Inc.

Printed in the United States of America

06 07 08 10 9 8 7 6 5 4 3 2 1

Library of Congress Cataloging-in-Publication Data

Lankford, Kimberly.
 The insurance maze : how you can save money on insurance—and still get the coverage you need / Kimberly Lankford.
    p. cm.
 Includes index.
 ISBN-13: 978-1-4195-2694-7
 ISBN-10:   1-4195-2694-4
 1. Insurance—United States. I. Title.
 HG8531.L35 2006
 368'.973—dc22
                          2006004533

Kaplan Publishing books are available at special quantity discounts to use for sales promotions, employee premiums, or educational purposes. Please call our Special Sales Department to order or for more information at 800-621-9621, ext. 4444, e-mail kaplanpubsales@kaplan.com, or write to Kaplan Publishing, 30 South Wacker Drive, Suite 2500, Chicago, IL 60606-7481.

DEDICATION

To Will and Houman

CONTENTS

Your entire financial plan is at risk if you do not have the right insurance. Without it, a split-second event could quickly wipe out the savings you've taken years to build.

Some of the biggest stories of the past few years emphasized the importance—and the challenges—of having the right insurance: the devastation of Hurricane Katrina and the victims' struggles to get their claims paid, the crisis in health insurance as rates exploded and employers slashed coverage, and the massive confusion surrounding the new Medicare prescription drug plan.

But if you know the right strategies, insurance can be affordable, accessible, and an incredibly powerful tool. It can protect your family against financial ruin from almost every situation that you worry about—a catastrophic illness, an auto accident, a disaster that damages your home, an expensive nursing home stay, or a death in the family.

Even though so much is at stake, people make big mistakes when shopping for insurance. They don't buy enough coverage, buy the wrong insurance, or pay hundreds—sometimes thousands—of dollars more than they should because they don't know how to deal with this complicated subject. As too many people learned after Hurricane Katrina, just having insurance may not be enough. You need to have the right type and amount of coverage.

But many people get cajoled into buying the wrong policy by a salesperson who is trying to earn a big commission, and regulators have recently uncovered several scandals involving inappropriate sales practices in many areas of the insurance business. It's tough to know who to trust when looking for insurance advice.

That is the reason I've always wanted to write this book. As a journalist covering insurance for more than a decade, I've been investigating the business from the inside and out—first writing about the industry for insurance executives, agents, and financial planners, then revealing the behind-the-scenes information to help consumers as the chief insurance writer for *Kiplinger's Personal Finance Magazine* and author of the popular Ask Kim column. In my columns and in this book, I cut through the hype, translate the technical language, and reveal the insider strategies that can help you get precisely the right coverage at the best price.

This is a particularly good time for everyone to review their insurance coverage. The entire insurance business has gone through tremendous changes over the past few years, and many of the buying strategies that worked in the past have already become outdated. For example:

- Despite the doomsday headlines about soaring health insurance costs, many people can get surprisingly good deals if they know how to make the most of their employers' options or shop around for a policy on their own. In addition, new tax benefits can help you cut your health insurance costs—and build a huge stash of money for future expenses.

- Most retirees were inundated with confusing choices when the new Medicare prescription drug plan was introduced. If you know about a few essential tools and shopping strategies, however, you can minimize the confusion and find a surprisingly affordable policy that lowers your drug costs significantly. Furthermore, if you made mistakes when initially selecting your policy, you still have plenty of time to make adjustments.

- After several tough years financially, most homeowners insurance companies have been raising rates at a double-digit pace and dropping customers who make just a few small claims. Now that insurers share information about you in a semisecret database, it's no longer safe to submit all claims that you can qualify for or switch insurers frequently to lower your premiums. Meanwhile, most people have way too little homeowners insurance and giant gaps in their coverage. After Hurricane Katrina, many people who had not updated their policies ended up with tens of thousands of dollars in expenses their insurance didn't cover.

- Life insurance rates have plummeted over the past decade, and almost everyone can lower their premiums now, or lock in the same rate for a longer time period, just by knowing how to shop around. Many people with medical conditions can finally get coverage even if they have been rejected in the past.

- Several large auto insurance companies are in the midst of making major pricing changes, which can cut premiums for people with good driving and credit records and provide more coverage options for riskier drivers who were shunned to special insurers in the past. Shopping around is essential. The price range can be huge from company to company and it isn't unusual for the insurer that offers your neighbor the lowest price to be the highest-priced option for you. Unless you double check an agent's recommendation, you could end up paying hundreds of dollars more than you need to every year.

- Long-term care insurance can protect you against the exorbitant costs of care in the future. The average rate for one year in a nursing home now exceeds $70,000 per year. If prices continue to rise by about 5 percent per year, then the average annual price tag could reach nearly $200,000 in 20 years. Adding to this problem is the fact that some large insurers ended up with big financial troubles when they started to pay nursing-home claims, and some left the business or unexpectedly raised rates for customers who had paid premiums for years—making the coverage unaffordable for many seniors on a limited income. You need to pick your benefits carefully and look for clues to a company's stability before buying a policy.

- Most people have way too little disability insurance through work, and even with the coverage you could end up with less than half your current income if you cannot do your job. If that isn't enough to pay your family's bills, then you should consider an individual disability insurance policy. It's incredibly complicated to shop for a policy, though, and one of the largest insurance companies has been hit with several multimillion dollar fines and lawsuits for its sales practices. You need to know exactly what you're looking for and how to shop carefully for a company before buying a policy.

This comprehensive guide focuses on the changes in every kind of insurance and the new strategies for finding a good deal. Each chapter highlights steps you can take to make the most of each type of coverage and avoid expensive mistakes that can jeopardize your family's financial plans. I'll conclude by putting it all into context and focusing on the key insurance moves you need to make during each stage of your life—whether you are just starting out, have a new baby, a teenage driver, an empty nest, or have finally retired. The information is very valuable: Understanding the new rules of insurance can help you free up thousands of dollars from your budget and protect your entire financial life at every stage of your life.

Nobody enjoys thinking about insurance, but you don't have a choice. Just hoping for the best or putting all of your faith in an insurance agent is a recipe for disaster. Read this book to help your family and yourself make the right decisions that are essential to your financial security.

CHAPTER 1

HEALTH INSURANCE

■ ■ ■

Health insurance has a greater impact on people's everyday lives than any other kind of insurance and almost any financial decision. People use it throughout the year, feel the pain of high premiums with every paycheck, and know that dropping the coverage could lead to financial disaster. A study by Harvard Law and Medical Schools found that nearly half of all Americans who file for bankruptcy do so because of medical expenses.

With such high stakes, it's no surprise that many people make major life decisions—when to retire, where to work, and where to live—based on access to health insurance. Some are even afraid to move, leave jobs they hate, or get divorced because they worry that they will lose their medical coverage.

To further complicate the situation, health insurance doesn't always provide as much protection as you'd expect. The biggest surprise from the Harvard study: Three-quarters of the people who filed for bankruptcy because of medical bills actually had health insurance. They still ended up with big bills because of high premiums, copayments, and gaps in coverage. Just having health insurance isn't enough anymore; choosing the right coverage at the right price is what makes the difference.

Many people, however, have no idea how to shop for health insurance. They never had to worry about the coverage—or medical expenses—as long as their employer covered a big chunk of the costs. Those costs, however, have exploded over the past few years.

Premiums for employee health insurance have risen by 73 percent since 2000, according to the Kaiser Family Foundation, with the average family plan costing $10,880 per year; $4,024 for singles. By contrast, inflation has increased by 14 percent and wage growth by 15 percent over the same time period. In fact, the average annual cost for a family plan is almost identical to the annual salary of someone working full-time for minimum wage. Most employers still cover part of the bill, but they are also cutting back on coverage and boosting costs in less obvious ways. When you add premiums plus increasing copayments, deductibles, and other expenses, people with employee coverage are paying about 125 percent more for their healthcare costs in 2005 than they were in 1999, according to Hewitt Associates, a human resources consulting firm—and those are the lucky ones.

The situation is even worse for people who retired early, lost their jobs, or started their own business and don't have coverage from an employer plan. The average 40-year-old pays $2,262 per year for single coverage and $4,146 for family coverage when buying health insurance on his own, according to a study by America's Health Insurance Plans, a trade association for health insurers. Unlike group coverage, they have to foot the entire bill themselves, and the price for individual health insurance varies enormously depending on your age, location, and medical condition. The average 60-year-old pays $4,185 per year for individual health insurance and $7,248 for family coverage, not including extra expenses for copayments and deductibles, which tend to be higher than they are in employer plans. Unhealthy people pay a lot more, or may have a tough time even finding coverage.

There is good news, however: Now is actually a great time to shop for health insurance. New tools make it a lot easier to compare your options, new types of policies can cut your premiums by hundreds or thousands of dollars, and new tax laws help you accumulate a tax-free stash of money to cover your medical expenses. It can be surprisingly easy and inexpensive for many people to buy health insurance on their own, and even people in poor health have many more options than they realize.

You can save a lot of money and find better coverage if you understand the changes insurers have been making behind the scenes and know what to look for in a policy. It isn't as simple as just switching to a lower-premium policy, which can actually increase your costs. Instead, you need to know how to hunt for hidden expenses and compare overall costs. Here are some strategies to help you find a better deal, whether you get health insurance through your employer or buy it on your own.

DEALING WITH EMPLOYER COVERAGE

Getting health insurance at work used to be a great deal. You would get coverage automatically—whether you were healthy or not—and the company paid the bulk of the bills. Many employees were blissfully ignorant of their healthcare costs because their employer picked up most of the tab.

That world has changed. Employee health insurance still has the big benefit of providing coverage regardless of your health, but both employers and employees have been feeling the pain of rising costs. Premiums for employee health insurance rose by more than 9 percent in 2005, following four years of double-digit growth from 2000 until 2004, according to the Kaiser Family Foundation. The average family plan costs $10,880 per year; $4,024 for singles.

Employers still subsidize most of the premiums, but everyone pays a lot more than they used to. The average employee pays $2,713 per year for family coverage (with employees at firms with fewer than 200 people paying $3,170 per year), according to the Kaiser study—and that's just a portion of the overall costs. Employers have been increasing deductibles, copayments, and other out-of-pocket expenses. The policy with the lowest premium may end up costing you the most by the end of the year.

People with employee coverage are notoriously bad at assessing their health insurance options. They generally pick a plan when they start a new job and automatically sign up again every year. That's a big mistake, especially right now. Employers have been making major changes to their health insurance offerings over the past few years. In addition to boosting premiums and out-of-pocket costs, they've been adding surcharges that can make it much more expensive to insure your family. The policy that worked best for you last year may now be one of your worst options. In fact, some employers' plans have become so expensive and limited that you may be able to get a much better deal by foregoing your employer's plan entirely and searching for coverage on your own. Meanwhile, some companies are adding valuable new options, such as health savings accounts, which can cut your premiums significantly and build up a tax-free saving account for medical expenses. You need to look at all of your choices before choosing a plan this year.

Learn how to compare hidden costs: The policy with the lowest premium may actually cost you the most.

Think you're having a tough time paying for health insurance? Your employer may be struggling even more than you are. Most employers still pay the bulk of employees' premiums, covering $8,167 of the bill for families; $3,413 for singles (see Figure 1.1). They've been covering about three-quarters of the bill for families since 1988, and haven't decreased the percentage even though costs have exploded since then.

That's all because of competition. Because health insurance is the most valuable employee benefit for many people, employers want to look like they're offering good coverage so they can attract and keep high-quality employees. It's easy to compare policies by premium, and it doesn't look good to boost the bill too much in one year, so employers are searching for less-obvious ways to control their costs. Don't be surprised to see higher deductibles and greater out-of-pocket costs for prescription drugs, doctor's visits, and hospital stays. You may not notice the price increases at first, but the extra costs add up. That's why employees are paying about 125 percent more for their healthcare costs in 2005 than they were in 1999, according to the Hewitt Associates study.

It's very important to look carefully at all of your health insurance options during open-enrollment season in the fall or whenever you switch jobs. Don't be surprised if the policy with the lowest premium actually ends up costing you the most by the end of the year.

You need to compare premiums and out-of-pocket costs for your family's typical medical and drug expenses, as well as the coverage caps for catastrophic care. Many employers have online tools to help you run the numbers. You may discover that the policy that cost the least in the past may no longer be your best option, and even after you pick a policy, you need to keep those cost-sharing increases in mind when choosing which doctors, hospitals, and prescription drugs to use. Because more money is coming out of your own pocket, it pays to become a smart healthcare consumer.

Many employers are boosting employees' healthcare costs in the following hidden ways:

- *Rising deductibles*—Most employer policies have a deductible, an amount the employee must pay out of his own pocket before the insurance kicks in. The average deductibles have increased significantly over the past few years—from $186 for single coverage in a preferred-provider organization in 1999, the most common type of plan, to $323 in 2005, according to the Kaiser Family Foundation. If you exclude the companies without a deductible, the average increases to $455 for single coverage and $952 for family coverage. A high deductible can be desirable if it lowers your premiums, too, but some employers are boosting their deductibles without giving you much savings, and keeping the money to lower their own costs.
- *Prescription drugs*—Many employees used to pay a fixed amount for all prescription drugs. Now they often have tiered

FIGURE 1.1 Average Annual Premiums for Covered Workers in 2005

Average Annual Premiums for Covered Workers in 2005—Single Coverage

	Worker Pays	Employer Pays	Total Cost
All Plans	$610	$3,413	$4,024
HMO	563	3,203	3,767
PPO	603	3,548	4,150

Average Annual Premiums for Covered Workers in 2005—Family Coverage

	Worker Pays	Employer Pays	Total Cost
All Plans	$2,713	$8,167	$10,880
HMO	2,604	7,852	10,456
PPO	2,641	8,449	11,090

Source: Kaiser/HRET Survey of Employer-Sponsored Health Benefits, 2005

pricing, charging a $10 copayment for a one month's supply of generic drugs, $21 for preferred drugs, and $33 for nonpreferred drugs. A few plans even have a fourth tier, with an average copayment of $74. Ask your doctor or pharmacist if you can switch to any generic or preferred drugs, which could save you a lot of money throughout the year. If you cannot avoid the highest-priced drugs, look very carefully at the prescription-drug coverage when comparing your plan options. It may be worthwhile to pay more in premiums in order to save money on drugs every month.

■ *Hospital stays*—You may have to pay extra money when you're admitted to the hospital, in addition to your regular deductibles and copayments. More than one-third of the people in the Kaiser Family Foundation study have to pay a separate deductible or copayment each time they're admitted to the hospital, with an average payment of $241. About 10 percent have to pay a separate coinsurance amount, at an average rate of 16 percent.

- *Doctor's visits*—Most workers now pay $15 to $20 per doctor's visit, but a few pay $25 or even $30. A small percentage pays even more, and that number is increasing. You may also see lower limits on the number of visits plans will cover for mental health and other types of specialized care—leaving you to cover the rest of those bills yourself.

- *Tiered costs*—A small but growing number of employers have several cost-sharing tiers for doctors and hospitals, based on their costs and quality, as they're doing with prescription drugs. More are considering the move in the future. Selecting a doctor or hospital based on its pricing tier can make a big difference in your out-of-pocket costs.

- *Shifting from copayments to coinsurance*—More companies are switching from a copay of a set dollar amount for doctor's visits and prescription drugs (often $15 to $25) and are charging coinsurance instead, where your out-of-pocket expenses are based on a percentage of the total cost. This change might look minor, but it can make a huge difference, especially for big-ticket items like expensive medications. With copays, actual price doesn't matter—few people think to ask about the total price if they know they'll just be paying $15. But it becomes essential to know the price when your costs are based on a percentage of the total costs. Companies are hoping that this move will encourage people to become better healthcare shoppers and lower their overall expenses, which will cut the bill for employees and the insurer.

- *Increasing out-of-pocket caps*—Potentially, the most damaging development for employees is any change in the out-of-pocket cap. Some insurance plans cover only 80 percent of your hospital costs and leave you to pay the remaining 20 percent—which could add up to thousands of dollars if you have a long stay. However, most plans protect you by capping your out-of-pocket expenses (your deductible plus copays) often at about

$5,000 for single coverage or $10,000 for families. A plan without this type of cap could leave you with tens of thousands of dollars in extra expenses if you have an expensive hospital stay.

■ *Shrinking coverage caps*—On the flip side, insurers generally have a maximum limit on the amount of coverage you can receive each year—often at $1 million or above. Some have much smaller limits, sometimes as low as $25,000 for first-year employees, or low limits on certain kinds of diseases. Again, you could end up with the entire bill beyond that amount—which could also cost you tens of thousands of dollars.

There are also the issues beyond the dollars. A health maintenance organization may have fewer out-of-pocket expenses throughout the year, but your primary-care physician generally acts as a gatekeeper, you can only use certain doctors and hospitals, and your coverage for non-emergencies will be limited when away from home. Coverage with a preferred-provider organization generally costs more, but you have more flexibility, too—you'll pay less if you use preferred doctors and hospitals, but can still see other doctors if you're willing to pay more. You need to decide whether the added flexibility is worth the extra money.

Your employer wants you to go away. It might be smart to take them up on that offer.

Even though employers are boosting your share of the costs, they're still paying the bulk of the bills themselves. A few have dropped health insurance entirely—69 percent of the companies surveyed by the Kaiser Family Foundation provided health insurance in 2000, but the number fell to 60 percent in 2005. Most companies, especially large ones (98 percent of firms with 200 or more workers provide health insurance), want to continue to offer health insurance as a competitive employee benefit. So instead of dropping the coverage, they're trying to encourage you and your family to choose to get your insurance somewhere else.

One of the big changes over the past few years—and a key reason not to blindly sign up for the plan you've always had—is that employers are starting to charge family members a lot more than employees for coverage. Employers have always treated their employees better than their employees' families—the average employer covers 84 percent of the total health insurance bill for individuals, for example, but only 74 percent of the cost of family coverage, an average subsidy that has changed very little over the past five years, according to the Kaiser Family Foundation. Employers want to continue to provide benefits to their employees, but cannot afford to help their families as much. In a 2004 Kaiser study, 41 percent of employers offering health benefits said they were likely to increase the percentage of the family premium that employees must pay in the next two years.

Employers are also adding more obvious incentives to get people to leave. Many are tacking on a surcharge—sometimes as much as $100 per month—if your family members have access to health insurance elsewhere (such as their own employers) but choose coverage from your employer's plan instead. Some firms even offer their employees bonuses if they decline the company's offer of health insurance.

These new developments make it essential for your family to compare all of your health insurance options before picking the best one. If both you and your spouse have employee coverage, you might want to stay on your employer's policy but shift your wife and kids to her employer's plan, or you may want to move the whole family to your company's insurance. Run the numbers for your potential costs (premiums plus other out-of-pocket expenses) for your regular medical bills, and compare the potential costs for catastrophic care. Be sure to factor in any bonuses or penalties for switching to another plan. The calculations may take a while, but they could save your family thousands of dollars in expenses throughout the year.

Sometimes it pays to turn down your employer's policy.

If your employer increases your premiums or out-of-pocket costs significantly, you may actually save money by buying your own insurance rather than staying with your employer's plan. A healthy 35-year-old man in California could buy a preferred-provider policy with a $1,000 deductible for about $888 per year or a $1,500 deductible for just $672 per year, according to insurance marketplace eHealthInsurance. If your employer boosts costs for family members a lot more than for employees, you may do better by staying on that plan yourself but buying individual coverage for your spouse and children.

This strategy only works if you're healthy and live in a state with a competitive health insurance marketplace. When employers offer health insurance, generally all employees are covered regardless of their medical condition. Because everyone pays the same price, the healthy people end up subsidizing the costs for the unhealthy people, who tend to have higher medical expenses. When you buy a policy on your own, however, the price (and ability to get coverage at all) can vary greatly depending on your age and health. Insurers generally give you extra credit if you're young and healthy, which is why individual health insurance policies tend to cost a lot less for them than the total cost of employer policies. The only reason why employees generally have a good deal is because most employers subsidize part of the cost.

The state you live in makes a big difference, too. In some states, like California, insurance companies can price the policies based on the insured's age and health condition. Because many insurers sell the coverage in the state, the prices tend to be particularly competitive for healthy people, but every state has different rules and a different marketplace. California has the lowest average premiums in the country at $1,885 for single coverage, according to a study by the America's Health Insurance Plans, an insurance-company trade group. Illinois lets insurers base costs on health and age, too, but the marketplace is a bit different—the average price there is $2,548.

Average prices skyrocket in states where insurers cannot reject anyone and must charge everyone the same price regardless of their health or age. In New York, where insurers can set rates by region, the average is $3,743, and it is $6,048 in New Jersey, where insurers must charge the same amount throughout the state.

Before you switch to an individual policy, however, make sure you aren't giving up important coverage. Some individual policies have exclusions and coverage limits that you may not have with your employer's policy. Compare total out-of-pocket costs for your expected medical expenses for the year and any caps on catastrophic costs, rather than just looking at premiums. Some individual plans, for example, may have limited coverage for pre-existing conditions, prescription drugs, or maternity care that may be a lot more restrictive than your employer's plan.

It's easy to shop around. You can get immediate price quotes for many companies, buy a policy, or talk with a licensed agent through eHealthInsurance (or call 800-977-8860 for personalized attention). You can find a health insurance agent in your area through the National Association of Health Underwriters (*www.nahu.org*). Ask the agent specifically if they work with individuals (some only work with groups) or if they can recommend someone else in your area who does. You can also contact the health insurance companies directly. Most state insurance department Web sites list contact information for companies offering health insurance in the area. The National Association of Insurance Commissioners Web site (*www.naic.org/state_web_map.htm*) provides links for each state regulator's Web site, which generally include pricing information and consumer-complaint ratings for insurers doing business in the state.

Keep in mind that the price will be a lot higher for the individual plan if you have any pre-existing medical conditions. Never drop your group policy before guaranteeing that you have coverage elsewhere, just in case it ends up being tougher to get the new policy than you were expecting.

Another tip: You may save money if you apply for an individual policy in November or early December, soon after you get the new pricing figures for your employer's plan. Most health insurers raise their rates on January 1, but if your policy is issued before New Year's Eve, you can lock in the previous year's rates for 12 months. Don't wait until the last minute—it generally takes about 30 days between when you apply for the policy and when it is issued.

Don't automatically keep your employer's COBRA coverage after you leave your job or get divorced.

A federal law, called the Consolidated Omnibus Budget Reconciliation Act (COBRA) requires companies with 20 or more employees to let you stay on their health insurance plan for up to 18 months after you leave your job. However, if you're healthy and live in a state with a competitive insurance marketplace, then you might find a much better deal on your own. That's because when you go on COBRA, you have to foot the entire bill yourself. If your employer had been subsidizing a big chunk of the cost, which most of them do, then your premiums could jump enormously—employees pay an average of $2,713 per year for family coverage, just about 26 percent of the total cost, but if you go on COBRA, you have to pay the full $10,880 yourself (plus up to 2 percent in administrative costs). The difference can be even bigger for people who have single coverage through their employer—they're paying an average of $610 themselves, just about 16 percent of the total cost, but have to pay the full $4,024 bill themselves on COBRA.

The best thing about COBRA is that you can continue the same coverage you had when you were an employee, so you don't need to change doctors, hospitals, or medications, and the insurance company cannot turn you down, regardless of your health status. If you do have any medical problems, staying on COBRA may be your best option.

If you're healthy, though, you could find a much better deal on your own. The average cost of an individual policy nationwide is $2,268, which is much less than the average $4,024 for single coverage under a group policy. The coverage may not be quite as comprehensive and the price (and availability) will vary depending on your health, but if you're generally healthy and live in a competitive state, you could almost cut the price in half. You'll save even more if you increase your deductible, which will lower your premiums and let you reap big tax benefits from a health savings account (discussed in more detail in the next section).

Because COBRA has very strict deadlines for signing up, though, it's very important to make sure you qualify for an individual policy before you turn down COBRA. If time is tight, go ahead and sign up for COBRA and keep it for a few months while you search for an individual policy, then don't drop that coverage until your own policy is up and running. This way you never go without insurance. Too many people think they're healthy, opt out of COBRA, and then scramble around to find coverage after they've been rejected by several individual insurers, or they get a new job with a waiting period before health benefits kick in, then end up with no coverage for a few months.

A similar strategy also applies if you get divorced. In that case, COBRA lets you keep coverage under your spouse's policy for up to 36 months, but you may also find a better deal on your own.

Raising your deductible brings huge savings—even more than you realize.

Raising your deductible can lower your premiums significantly and give you more control over your healthcare costs.

Psychologically, raising your deductible from $500 to $1,000 might not seem like much of a bargain because you have to pay more money out of your own pocket before the insurance kicks in. The value depends on how much money you're saving in premiums and how many medical expenses you end up having throughout the year.

According to eHealthInsurance, a 35-year-old male in Chicago, for example, could cut his annual premiums down from $1,700 to $1,452, by raising his deductible from $500 to $1,000. The equation is even better if raising your deductible ends up saving you exactly the same amount of money in premiums—a $500 premium reduction, for example, in return for raising your deductible by $500— which it does in many cases, and that's just part of the savings. Most people will come out even further ahead because they generally do not spend up to the full deductible. In that case, if you raise your deductible from $500 to $1,000, for example, but only end up using $600 in medical expenses, you could save $500 in premiums and only spend an extra $100 out of your own pocket.

That isn't even counting the tax savings. In 2006, if you raise your deductible to $1,050 for a single policy or $2,100 for family policies, you may also be eligible for a health savings account, which can give you valuable tax benefits.

Check out new options: Opening a health savings account can lower your premiums, save big money in taxes, and help you build up a huge retirement stash.

The most exciting new development in health insurance is the health savings account (HSA), which is another big reason not to automatically stick with the policy you've always had. HSAs were introduced in 2004, but many employers had already made their health insurance decisions for the year and didn't offer them until 2005, when 7 percent of employers offered the plans. That number is expected to increase to 32 percent in 2006, according to Mellon's Human Resources & Investor Solutions. If your employer offers an HSA, it could be a great way to cut down on your health insurance costs. It's also one of the rare ways to save money tax-free regardless of your income level—whether you get insurance through your employer or on your own.

In order to open an HSA, you must not be enrolled in Medicare (which means you generally need to be under age 65) and your health insurance policy must have a deductible of at least $2,100 for a family policy in 2006 (or $1,050 for an individual policy) and meet a few other requirements. Then, you can get a triple tax break. You can set aside tax-deductible money in an HSA up to the amount of the deductible, with a maximum, in 2006, of $5,450 for families or $2,700 for individuals (people age 55 or older can contribute an extra $700 in 2006). You can withdraw the money tax-free at any time to pay for medical expenses. Unlike a flexible-spending account, another tax-free plan that many employers offer to pay for medical expenses, you do not need to use the money by the end of the year. Any money you don't spend right away can remain in the account for future expenses. You can use the money tax-free at any age for medical bills, or you can use it for any reason after age 65 without paying a penalty, although withdrawals for nonmedical expenses will be taxed. Before age 65, if you withdraw money for nonmedical expenses, you'll owe income tax and a 10 percent penalty.

You can keep the plan even if you change jobs, and contribution amounts aren't limited based on your income (like they are with many retirement plans). It's one of the few ways that even high-income people can get triple tax savings—with contributions lowering their current income, growing tax-deferred, and available tax-free for medical expenses anytime in the future.

You can either have an HSA-eligible policy through your employer or buy the coverage on your own. The employer or insurer may pair your HSA-eligible policy with a health savings account, or you can open up an account with a bank or other financial institution.

So far, HSAs have been most popular with people who are self-employed or buy their own health insurance. Because they've been paying the full cost of health insurance themselves, without any employer subsidy, many already had high-deductible policies as a way to make their premiums more manageable. If you're on your own, switching to an HSA can be an easy way to lower your premiums, cut your current tax bill, and accumulate a tax-free stash for future medical expenses.

You can deduct your HSA contributions from your taxable income—whether or not you itemize deductions. If you're in the 25 percent federal tax bracket, contributing $3,000 to an HSA will lower your federal tax bill by $750. Another way to look at it: Contributing $3,000 per year to an HSA through your employer will only lower your paycheck by $2,250. Then you can use that money tax-free for medical expenses in any year—a double-whammy of a tax benefit that is nearly impossible to find anywhere else.

To decide whether a high-deductible policy with an HSA is right for you, you need to compare your potential out-of-pocket expenses (premiums, deductibles, and copays, plus the tax advantages) to your other options. If you're buying health insurance on your own, a high-deductible health plan with an HSA is usually your best bet. If you're getting health insurance through your employer, you need to look at the overall package. Some small companies are offering it as their only health insurance plan, but larger companies are including it among their menu of options. Some may be passing along the premium savings to employees and even contributing some money into their health savings accounts. Workers enrolled in HSA-eligible policies, on average, receive an annual employer contribution to their HSA of $533 for single coverage and $1,185 for family coverage, according to the Kaiser Family Foundation. Other employers, however, are raising deductibles as a way to cut down their own health insurance costs—but not reducing employees' premiums by nearly as much—and about one-third of the employers offering HSA-eligible policies didn't contribute anything to their employees' accounts. You'll need to compare the total deal to your other health insurance options.

To make the most of your HSA, toss the debit card and don't use the money for current medical expenses.

You can use the money in a health savings account tax-free for any out-of-pocket medical expenses permitted under federal law, which includes most medical, dental, and vision care, as well as pre-scription and over-the-counter drugs for yourself, your spouse, and your dependent children. The HSA money can even be used for some expenses that aren't covered by your health insurance policy, such as braces, glasses, and aspirin. Many insurers try to make it easy to use your HSA money by giving you a debit card.

You will only reap the maximum benefits if you toss the debit card and keep the money in the account. That means not touching it for current medical expenses—using other cash for those costs and keeping the HSA money in the account for as long as possible. Keeping the money in the account can make the most of the tax benefits and help you build a tax-free fund for future medical expenses.

Consider this: If you contribute the money to the HSA each year, you will be able to lower your current tax bill. Investing $3,000 per year, for example, will lower your federal income-tax bill by $750 if you're in the 25 percent bracket, but you'll get even bigger tax benefits if you keep the money in the account for the long run.

If you start investing $3,000 per year into the HSA when you're 35, earn 8 percent per year, and don't touch the money for 30 years, you'll have about $360,000 by age 65. You could use the money for anything at that point without a penalty and you will only have to pay income taxes on the money, or you can use it for medical expenses at any age, before or after age 65, and never owe taxes on the money—which is a much better deal. The longer you keep the money in the account, the more you will benefit from the tax-free growth.

The money can come in handy to help pay for medical expenses if you retire early, and even though you can't contribute new money to an HSA after age 65, you'll still have plenty of eligible medical expenses even after you qualify for Medicare. You can use HSA money to pay premiums for Medicare Parts A, B, C and prescription drug coverage Part D, Medicare copays, deductibles, and other out-of-pocket expenses, and qualified long-term care insurance. You cannot, however, use the money to pay Medicare supplement-insurance premiums.

If you do plan to use other money for current medical expenses, you need to make sure you keep enough money in your emergency fund so you aren't caught off-guard if you end up with big medical bills. Cash flow is the biggest difference between high-deductible and low-deductible policies. With a low-deductible policy, you pay a fixed (but higher) amount every month and have few surprise expenses throughout the year. With a high-deductible policy, your premiums are lower, but you never know when you may have an emergency and have to pay a few thousand dollars yourself in medical expenses. The entire HSA savings strategy will backfire if you have to go in debt or sell stocks at an inopportune time in order to come up with the cash to pay the bills.

Keep enough money to cover your deductible in a guaranteed account that is easy to access, such as a money-market account or a money-market fund. You can search for good rates for money-market accounts at *www.bankrate.com* or for money-market funds at *www.imoneynet.com.*

HSA fees and bad investments can eat up all of the tax benefits. Search for a cheap HSA—and keep shopping for better deals.

If you're keeping your HSA money in the account for the long run, you need to find investments to match your timeframe. That can be surprisingly difficult to do. Anticipating that most employees will use the money for medical costs each year, the first wave of HSA providers only offered fixed-interest accounts, paying about 3 percent per year. They kept the cash in a money-market account so it would be accessible if you needed it right away for medical costs. If you plan on building up your HSA stash for long-term savings, however, then you'll need investments to match.

Long-term investments should generally be in stocks or stock funds, and it had been tough to find HSA administrators that let you invest in funds. More banks and financial institutions are starting to offer HSA accounts now and they're gradually improving their investment choices. A few now offer full brokerage options, which let you invest in funds as well as stocks.

However, you need to be very careful about fees. There's a big range in fees, and some are so high that they erase the benefits of the HSAs—especially for people who keep the money in a low-interest account and spend it throughout the year on medical expenses. A study of 90 banks by HSAfinder.com found that the fees charged for HSA accounts ranged from $0 to $238 per year, with an average of $50.

As more people boost their balances in the HSA accounts, competition should improve investment choices and drive down fees. Few low-cost mutual fund providers have entered the market so far—you can only get Vanguard funds through a few third-party providers and not directly from the company. Fidelity launched a very limited pilot program with a few employers, which it expects to expand in the next few years.

As competition improves, continue to search for better options from HSA administrators. Keep an eye out for new developments and switch when you find a better deal. Shifting from one HSA provider to another should eventually become as easy as making an IRA rollover. You won't face a penalty or tax bill as long as you make a direct transfer from one administrator to another and don't touch the money yourself. The administrator you're switching to should be able to walk you through the process—they're usually excited to get your money and make the transition as easy as possible.

You can shop for an HSA administrator at HSA Insider (*www.hsainsider.com*) and HSA Finder (*www.hsafinder.com*). If you have an HSA-eligible policy through an employer, they may automatically set you up with an HSA administrator, which may be a lot easier to stick with, especially if the employer is contributing to your account and is covering some of the fees. Otherwise, you should be able to use whichever administrator you want, and it's a good idea to check out the alternatives instead of automatically keeping your health savings account with the company that provides your health insurance.

You'll only save money if you become a smart healthcare shopper.

In the old days, when deductibles were low and copayments were nonexistent, most people had no idea how much their medical care actually cost. They'd pay their premium and the insurance company picked up the tab as long as the treatment was covered. Now that insurers are raising deductibles and boosting your share of out-of-pocket costs, you have a big incentive to spend less money on your medical care. If you have to shell out the first $3,000 in medical expenses before your insurance kicks in, you're probably a lot less likely to go to the emergency room with a question you could get answered over the phone—especially if you get to keep the money you save in a tax-advantaged health savings account—and if you're paying a percentage of the cost for your medications, you'll generally be more motivated to ask your doctor or pharmacist about generic alternatives. Insurers are hoping those moves will help lower their costs, too.

You'll save a lot of money by becoming a smart healthcare shopper, but because it's a totally different mindset most people still have no idea how much medical care costs or how to shop for it. A study by Great-West Healthcare shows how ignorant many people still are about their medical expenses, especially if they get their insurance through work. The people surveyed had employer-sponsored health insurance and could guess the cost of a new Honda Accord within 1 percent, and the price of a round-trip plane ticket in coach class from New York to Los Angeles within 8 percent, but made big mistakes when asked about medical costs—they were 20 percent off on the average cost of a routine doctor's office visit (it's $139), 24 percent off on the cost of an emergency room visit (it's $500), and made huge errors when guessing how much an average four-day hospital stay costs (they said $6,400, when it's actually $14,500).

Consumers also had a tough time understanding how much the cost of care can vary, for example, the cost of a 24-hour hospital stay can vary up to 60 percent by location (the people had guessed it was 20 percent). They did a much better job of estimating prescription drug costs, because many have to pay those expenses themselves.

Most people aren't used to asking questions about cost, either. Only 15 percent of the people surveyed learned the cost of their treatment before it occurred, 63 percent learned of it after the treatment, and 10 percent never found out the cost.

Simply asking how much a procedure costs isn't as easy as it sounds. Because doctors and hospitals negotiate different rates with different insurance companies, there isn't always one fixed rate that's easy for your doctor's receptionist to rattle off. Some insurers, however, are offering tools to help people shop. Aetna, for example, is giving customers online access to the discounted rates for up to 25 of the most common office-based services offered by their physicians—information that can be difficult to track down on your own. Other insurers rank hospitals based on cost and quality of care.

Other strategies that can help you lower your medical expenses:

- *Meet with your doctor or pharmacist to review all of your medications.* Find out whether you can switch to lower-cost or generic medications and whether you've been prescribed any duplicate medicines by different doctors.
- *Investigate cheaper ways to buy your medications.* Look into using a mail-order pharmacy, buying in bulk, or shopping around for a lower-cost pharmacy. Also ask your doctor for strategies or special deals, and visit the BenefitsCheckUp Web site at *www.benefitscheckup.com* (the version for people who aren't on Medicare) for information about state pharmacy assistance programs and other resources that can help

you pay for your medications, especially if you fall below
certain income levels.

■ *Look for alternatives for basic medical supplies.* Buying
crutches yourself at a medical-supply store, for example, may
cost a lot less than taking them home from the hospital.

■ *Make the most of your insurer's medical help.* More are offering 24-hour help lines, staffed by nurses that can often
answer basic questions and help you avoid a trip to the doctor
or emergency room. Some have online resources with a lot of
information to help with your diagnosis. Don't go overboard
trying to save money, though—it can be dangerous to avoid
a trip to the doctor or emergency room when you really do
need immediate medical help.

■ *Take advantage of free preventive care.* Insurers realize that
the healthier you are, the less you'll end up costing them.
HMOs were always big into preventive care, but now all
kinds of insurers are providing incentives to get you to live a
healthier life, which can give you some extra cash, free coverage, and should help lower your overall medical expenses.

Some employers give out cash bonuses if you take a health-risk
appraisal, follow a healthy lifestyle plan, or follow through on a
smoking-cessation program. More than half the covered workers in
the Kaiser Family Foundation study are in a plan with at least one
disease management program, such as for diabetes, asthma, hypertension, or high cholesterol. These programs teach patients about the
disease, suggest treatment options, and assess their progress. Many
large firms offer fitness programs or on-site health clubs, and programs to help people stop smoking, prevent injuries, and lose weight,
and quite a few companies now cover 100 percent of preventive care
with no deductible, paying the full cost of annual physicals, routine
prenatal and well-child care, adult immunizations, mammograms,
and pap smears.

HEALTH INSURANCE WHEN YOU'RE ON YOUR OWN

Self-employed people, early retirees, and people without full-time jobs are used to shopping for health insurance and paying the bills themselves, and they're getting more company, as employers continue to drop health insurance coverage and leave employees to fend for themselves in the health insurance marketplace. Although 98 percent of all companies with 200 or more workers offer health insurance to employees, only 59 percent of firms with fewer than 200 workers offer the employee benefit (down from 68 percent in 2000), according to the Kaiser Family Foundation study.

Buying your own health insurance is often more expensive than employer policies because the boss doesn't subsidize the costs, but it doesn't cost as much as many people expect. You can find some surprisingly good deals if you know how to shop and what to look for in a policy.

Surprise! Buying your own health insurance generally costs a lot less than you'd expect.

So many people stay in jobs they don't like or won't start their own businesses because they're afraid of what will happen if they lose their employer's health insurance. They assume it will be incredibly expensive to get individual insurance. That's a huge mistake. The big secret: Most people have no idea how easy and affordable it can be to buy an individual health insurance policy if you're relatively healthy.

The average individual policy costs $2,268 for single coverage, instead of an average $4,024 for the full cost under an employer policy (see Figure 1.2). That's because most insurers can base their prices for individual coverage on the person's age and medical condition, which they generally can't do for employer coverage. Because employers must charge everyone the same amount, the

FIGURE 1.2 National Average Premiums by Age

Age	Average Premium Single	Average Premium Family
18–24	$1,170	$2,459
25–29	1,345	2,844
30–34	1,608	3,354
35–39	1,826	3,677
40–44	2,262	4,146
45–49	2,638	4,541
50–54	3,173	5,297
55–59	3,775	6,253
60–64	4,185	7,248
Total	2,268	4,424

*The average family has 2.12 to 3.39 members depending on the age group.
Source: Center for Policy and Research, America's Health Insurance Plans

healthy workers often end up paying more than required to cover their own risk, which helps cover the costs for the unhealthy workers. Employer plans can be a good deal for older people with health problems, but young and healthy people can generally find a good deal on their own—especially if they increase their deductible and have few medical expenses throughout the year. In addition, the introduction of health savings accounts has been a huge improvement for people who buy individual coverage. Most already boosted their deductibles as a way to lower their costs; now they get a tax benefit for that decision, too.

A healthy 35-year-old man in California can find an individual policy with a $1,000 deductible for $888 per year, or $672 per year for a $1,500 deductible, according to eHealthInsurance. The prices do vary a lot by state, because of differences in the laws and market-place. California has the lowest average costs for individual coverage in the country. The prices in Illinois, on the other hand, are slightly above average. In Chicago, a 35-year-old man could buy a policy with a $1,000 deductible for $1,452 per year. A 35-year-old couple with a two-year-old child could find a policy with a $2,000 deductible for $2,544 per year, according to eHealthInsurance.

The prices for individual coverage do rise as you get older—especially if your health deteriorates—which is the biggest problem with individual health insurance in most states. A 45-year-old Chicago couple with two teenage kids could find a policy with a $2,000 deductible for $6,256 per year, but a healthy 60-year-old couple would pay even more than that—$6,600 per year—for a policy just covering the two of them after their kids move out on their own.

Shopping around can make a huge difference. Why pay $8,000 when you can get the exact same coverage for $2,500?

Because health insurance is so complicated—and the coverage can vary so much—it's essential to shop around for an individual policy and get price quotes from several companies. The price range can be huge. A healthy 35-year-old couple with a two-year-old child in California could pay anywhere from $2,544 per year for a policy with a $2,000 deductible up to more than $8,000 for a similar policy, and those price variations aren't based on any differences in the family's health; it's just the range in prices from company to company.

You cannot just compare premiums, though, because insurers can hide price increases by raising copayments and other out-of-pocket expenses. You need to look carefully at the policy details, calculating the potential costs for your family for the year, and comparing any exclusions and caps for catastrophic coverage.

You can shop for individual policies with several companies from eHealthInsurance or find a local agent through the National Association of Health Underwriters (*www.nahu.org*) or get a list of companies selling health insurance in your state from your health insurance department (you can find links at the National Association of Insurance Commissioners Web site, *www.naic.org/state_web_map.htm*). You can also find lists of HSA-eligible policies at *www.hsainsider.com* or *www.hsadecisions.org.* Compare prices and coverage for a few companies before making a final decision, but do some prescreening before you start filling out applications to get an idea which ones are likely to insure you. Getting rejected by one company can make it tougher to find coverage with another.

Recent graduates have better options than COBRA.

Your kids can usually stay on your family policy while they're full-time students, generally up to age 25 (the rules vary by company). Then they can stay on your policy for up to 36 months on COBRA after they leave school or reach the cut-off age, but they'll generally get a better deal if they buy an individual policy, especially if they're healthy and don't live in New York or New Jersey.

Recent graduates have several alternatives, even if they don't find a job with benefits right after they graduate. If they plan in advance, they may be able to sign up for a student health policy that continues after they graduate. The costs are low—a 22-year-old male in Chicago could pay $624 per year ($52 per month) for a student policy with a $2,500 deductible (you can shop for student policies through eHealthInsurance, get quotes for Assurant Health's policy at *www.assurantstudentinsurance.com,* or contact the school or your state insurance department about other options). You cannot wait until the last minute, though, because many of these policies require you to be a full-time student for at least 31 days after the policy takes effect. These policies tend to have several limitations, however, such as no coverage for dependents, pregnancy, or outpatient prescription drugs. You must not have any major medical problems, and preexisting conditions may not be covered for 12 months.

In many cases, though, it's most cost-effective to sign up for a regular individual policy, which you can buy at any time—whether or not you're a student. These policies generally have fewer exclusions than the student health plans, and the price may be quite similar, depending on your medical condition and location. For example, a healthy 22-year-old male in Chicago could get an individual policy with a $2,750 deductible through eHealthInsurance for just $780 per year ($65 per month) or $1,037 ($86 per month) per year for a policy with a $1,000 deductible.

The individual policy can provide an added bonus: If you choose a policy that has at least a $1,050 deductible in 2006 for single coverage ($2,100 for families) and meets a few other requirements, then you can sign up for a health savings account that can lower your tax bill and accumulate a tax-free stash for future medical expenses or retirement. (You cannot, however, set up an HSA for a child who can be claimed as a dependent on your tax return.)

If cash is tight for your son or daughter—which it generally is for 22-year-olds—mom and dad can give the child money to contribute to the account. The money can pay medical expenses now or, much more valuable, can remain in the account and be a head start on retirement. Contributing $1,500 into an HSA starting at age 22 and continuing with the habit for the next 43 years, without touching the money, could yield more than $530,000 in the account by the time they're age 65 if their investments average 8 percent per year. At that time, they can use the money tax-free for medical expenses or with a tax bill—but no penalty—for anything they desire. That's a huge head start on retirement! Even if you just invest $1,500 now and never add more money to the account, the funds could eventually grow to more than $40,000 by age 65 if the investments earn 8 percent per year.

If, however, your child is about to start a job with health benefits, you may only want coverage to last a few months. In that case, you may want to consider a short-term health insurance policy. These policies are generally available for only 180 or 365 days, you cannot have any major medical problems, and they usually don't provide coverage for pregnancy, preventive care, or preexisting conditions. A 22-year-old man in Chicago could pay about $75 per month for a short-term policy with a $2,500 deductible. Assurant Health (*www.assuranthealth.com*), Golden Rule (*www.goldenrule.com*), and several Blue Cross/Blue Shield plans offer short-term policies, which can also be helpful for anyone who is between jobs. You can also get price quotes for several short-term policies through eHealth-Insurance.

Even if one of these options seems like a better deal than COBRA, it's important to sign your child up for COBRA first and don't drop that coverage until you are guaranteed that they have coverage elsewhere. Way too many children who think they are healthy forego COBRA then have troubles finding a job with benefits or have a waiting period for benefits at their new job, or end up with a medical condition that makes it difficult to get a good deal on individual insurance (even having attention deficit disorder can cause a rejection at some companies). You can drop COBRA when they get the new coverage, but it's important to know you have something to fall back on until you have an alternative locked in.

Early retirees can give themselves a great head start with an HSA.

Early retirees who don't have coverage through their former employers have some of the toughest times finding health insurance. Costs for individual insurance are steep when you're in your 50s and 60s, even if you are in excellent health. If you have any medical problems, the price of health insurance can be astronomical—if you can get it at all. A study by America's Health Insurance Plans, a trade association of health insurers, found that less than 12 percent of the health insurance applications for people ages 25 to 29 were denied, while 30 percent were denied for applicants ages

60 to 64. Some of these applicants ended up finding coverage through another insurer, even after being rejected. Slightly more than half of the accepted applicants ages 60 to 64 paid standard rates. The rest of the applicants were charged extra or had certain conditions excluded because of their health, and were reduced to counting down the days until they turned age 65 and could get low-cost coverage through Medicare.

Because it can be so tough to get coverage at this age, it's very important to sign up for COBRA when you leave your job. You can keep that coverage for up to 18 months and, even though this will cost a lot more than your share of the premiums as an employee, at least you know you have some coverage and the doctors, hospitals, and rules won't change.

It can be worthwhile to shop around for individual coverage if you're in good health, especially because COBRA runs out after just 18 months. The average premium is $4,185 for people ages 60 to 64 getting single coverage and $7,248 for family coverage, according to America's Health Insurance Plans.

If you buy a policy with a deductible of at least $1,050 for individual coverage, or $2,100 for families in 2006, then you may qualify for a health savings account, which can save you even more money. You'll be able to use that money tax-free for medical expenses at any age or penalty-free for anything after age 65 (you will have a tax bill for nonmedical expenses).

You will also be getting the biggest bang from your buck if you keep the money in the account for a few years so it can grow tax-deferred for a while, then use it for medical expenses rather than other retirement costs. If you start contributing $3,000 per year into an HSA when you're age 55, and your investment returns an average of 8 percent, you could accumulate about $45,000 by age 65.

Even after you become eligible for Medicare at age 65, you can still use your HSA money for plenty of medical expenses, including your Medicare premiums and out-of-pocket expenses such as deductibles and copays for Medicare Parts A, B, C, or D. You can also use the money to pay for qualified long-term care insurance, but you cannot use it for Medicare supplement premiums. For more tips on minimizing your medical expenses after age 65, see Chapter 2.

If you can't find affordable coverage, consider moving to another state.

There are two big problems with individual health insurance: You may not qualify for coverage at all if you have any medical problems, and the price varies enormously from state to state. Part of the reason for the variation is because medical costs can vary a lot in different parts of the country, but the biggest reason is the way that insurance is regulated. Each state has different rules for health insurers about how they can set rates, who they can accept and reject, and what they need to cover. Some states, like New York and New Jersey, require health insurers to cover everyone regardless of their health (called "guaranteed issue"), and charge the same rate regardless of their age (New York lets them adjust prices by region; New Jersey requires them to be the same for everyone). That means a 25-year-old marathoner will pay the same price as a 63-year-old who's had several heart surgeries.

The deal can be beneficial for someone in poor health—at least they will have some coverage—but a healthy person would pay much more in those states than they would anywhere else, and generally have fewer choices because many insurers decide not to sell insurance in those markets at all.

Most other states let insurers set their rates based on your age and medical condition, and young healthy people in those states will pay a lot less than they would in a guaranteed-issue state. A 35-year-old man in California could pay $888 for a policy with a $1,000 deductible in California, but the exact same man would end up paying more than $4,000 in New York. The deductibles in New York are generally a lot lower (this policy has a $0 deductible) but not nearly enough to make up for the price difference, and keep in mind that a 60-year-old man who had three heart surgeries would pay that same amount in New York.

New York does have some special policies for people with low incomes who earn too much to qualify for Medicaid. A family of three must earn less than $40,100 per year ($23,800 for singles) and meet several other criteria to qualify for the Healthy NY policy, which is offered by several companies and can cost around $2,200 per year for single coverage in New York City, or more than $6,000 for a family, about a third of the price they'd pay on the regular plan.

You can get a lot of helpful information on these policies, and price quotes for insurers throughout the state, at the state insurance Web site (*www.ins.state.ny.us*).

It doesn't hurt to check out health insurance prices before you move to a new state if you'll need to buy the coverage on your own. A healthy person will pay a lot less, for example, in nearby Connecticut or Pennsylvania. The opposite strategy can work if you're in poor health. In that case, you might find a better deal in a state with guaranteed issue laws, where it's illegal for insurers to turn you down.

One company may reject you while another offers a great rate.

In many states, the reason young, healthy people can get a good deal on individual health insurance is because insurers can charge them lower rates due to the smaller risk they pose to them. The opposite also holds true: In those same states, insurers can charge people with poor health a lot more or decide not to cover them at all. That's the biggest problem with individual insurance; the prices can be astronomical if you're old and unhealthy.

In addition, "unhealthy" can have a much broader definition than you might think. Some companies will deny people for surprising conditions like seasonal allergies and attention deficit disorder. Each insurer has very different definitions of health, and the results can range enormously from company to company.

If you have any health problems—even if they seem minor to you—it's usually best to work with an agent who deals with several companies and knows from experience which company is likely to accept you and offer the best deal. That's a lot easier than the trial-and-error strategy of applying everywhere yourself and it helps you avoid getting a rejection on your file, which often leads other companies to reject you as well. You can find an agent in your area through the National Association of Health Underwriters (*www.nahu.org*) or call eHealthInsurance (800-977-8860) to talk with an agent there rather than filling out the online quote form.

An experienced agent can also direct you to a company that's likely to offer the best deal for someone with your medical condition because the rules (and rates) vary significantly from company to company. Some may accept you but exclude the condition (unless state law mandates the coverage) and/or raise your rate, often from 25 percent to 300 percent above the price for healthy people. Shopping around is essential because it is not unusual for one company to accept you without any restrictions while another rejects you entirely.

One insurer may cover someone with hypertension as long as it is controlled with one medication, for example, while another may permit two medications. A third may only issue a policy after the condition has been under control for at least a year. Each insurer also has different height and weight requirements.

Insurers occasionally change their minds after rejecting you if you present a strong enough case, which may be easier to do if you're working with a health insurance agent who is familiar with the insurer's underwriting department. It also helps to provide information from your doctor about how you've managed your condition.

If your condition is relatively minor, you may be more likely to get accepted if you ask for a higher deductible, such as if you're on blood pressure or cholesterol medication and controlling your condition, so the insurer knows it won't be paying so much in prescription costs for you.

Don't be tempted to omit information on your application. Insurers check your medical records and will be more likely to reject you if they find out you're lying or, even worse, may deny your coverage retroactively later on—after you've built up medical bills.

Be sure to let the insurer know if your medical situation has improved. Sometimes an insurer will add a rate increase of 25 percent to 300 percent for a particular condition, and will remove the rate increase if several years have passed since you had the problem. They'll commonly do this, for example, if you had high blood pressure but the condition has been controlled for 24 months. You usually need to notify the company yourself—you cannot expect them to remove it automatically.

There's generally hope, even if you've been rejected.

Even if you've been rejected, keep shopping around—another insurer might consider your condition differently. Even if a few companies have rejected you, there's still hope in most parts of the country. In that case, you might be able to find coverage if your state is one of the 33 offering a high-risk pool, which will insure everyone, regardless of their medical condition.

The rules vary a lot from state to state: In some, you can only get coverage during certain times of the year; in others you need to prove you've been denied by either one or two insurance companies. Most states have a limit on the premiums the pools can charge, generally 125 percent to 150 percent higher than standard coverage. For more information, see the Communicating for Agriculture and the Self-Employed's high-risk pool Web site (*www.selfemployedcountry.org/riskpools.html*). This organization, which started by helping self-employed farmers in Minnesota find insurance, is now one of the best sources for information about state high-risk pools. Your state insurance department should also have information about your options, as well as the National Association of State Comprehensive Health Insurance Plans (*www.naschip.org*), the national organization for state health insurance pools.

Be very careful before moving to Florida, Arizona, or Nevada without health insurance.

A few states do not have open high-risk pools or guaranteed issue laws, however. That's when it gets particularly difficult for people with medical conditions to find coverage. Florida's high-risk pool, for example, hasn't been accepting people since about 1990, making it difficult for some people to buy a policy there at any price.

It's very important to find out about your health insurance situation before moving to Florida, Arizona, or Nevada, three popular retirement destinations that don't have an open pool for high-risk people. A local agent can explain the rules and your options, and you can also get a lot of helpful information from the state insurance department.

Many people inadvertently give up access to coverage because they don't know about their state's consumer protections. In Florida, for example, insurers must generally offer you a continuation policy as long as you didn't have a 63-day break in coverage, but not all types of policies qualify. It's also one of the few states that let you buy a group policy if you're self-employed, even if you don't have any other employees (most states require a group of at least two people), although the options are limited and the prices can be quite high. The high price, though, is better than going uninsured, which could leave you with much larger bills.

If you live in a state without a high-risk pool, it's essential to sign up for COBRA and keep that coverage until you know you have another option—even if you consider yourself to be healthy. Otherwise, you may be rejected for something you hadn't expected and end up with no insurance. If you go without insurance for more than 63 days, you may have a tough time finding new coverage; in many cases, insurers must provide you with some type of insurance as long as you've had continuous coverage. Because COBRA expires after 18 months, give yourself plenty of time before the deadline to research the alternatives in your state and find out what you need to do to qualify for a conversion policy.

Even if the premiums are very high, at least early retirees can be relieved that this is only a time-limited problem. As soon as they reach 65, they'll have low-cost coverage through Medicare, regardless of their medical condition.

Association plans can be a bad deal.

In a desperate search to find affordable health insurance, some people are lured to association group policies that seem to cost a lot less than their other options. In some cases, these policies can offer a good deal, helping people band together to get group discounts. You need to be very careful, though. These plans can sometimes be a good deal in the first year, but then prices rise and the healthy people leave, leaving the sicker people to remain in the group. As a result, prices rise even more (a problem that rarely happens with employee plans because both the workers in good and bad health usually stay with the group coverage). Check out the group's track record and compare prices to individual policies, which may have better coverage and more consumer protections. If an association plan offers an unusually low rate, make sure it is licensed with the state insurance department and check the policy carefully for coverage exclusions.

Some association group plans have even bigger problems. A study by Georgetown University's Health Policy Institute found that in many cases association health plans are not subject to the same regulations as individual and employer health insurance policies, and have been attracting scam artists. Between 2000 and 2002, state investigators shut down 41 illegal operations selling coverage through phony and real associations. In the worst cases, they set up fake health insurance plans for real trade associations—or sometimes create associations just to offer seemingly cheap health insurance—then leave employees with unpaid claims.

Be very wary if an association health plan is offering unusually low premiums, asking few medical questions, or is working with an association you've never heard of, especially if the association doesn't seem to have any purpose other than to provide health insurance. Also, check out the plan with your state insurance regulator to see if they've had any problems in the past and make sure they're subject to the same consumer protections as other insurers.

TIPS FOR GETTING THE RIGHT HEALTH INSURANCE AT THE BEST PRICE

Health insurance prices have been rising rapidly, but a few key strategies can help you get a good deal:

- Don't automatically sign up for the same employer health insurance plan you've always had. Employers have been making big changes to their health insurance options in attempts to lower their costs, such as raising premiums, cutting back coverage, and boosting deductibles and other out-of-pocket expenses. The policy with the lowest premiums may end up costing you the most by the end of the year. You need to run the numbers through your potential expenses for the upcoming year to determine which policy is best for your family.
- Many employers are offering incentives to encourage you and your family to get your health insurance elsewhere, such as offering bonuses if you don't sign up for your employer's plan or surcharges if your family could get coverage some-

where else but signs up for your policy instead. Check out all of your coverage options, such as insuring your whole family on your employer's policy, switching everyone to your spouse's employer plan, or staying on your employer's plan yourself while your spouse and kids go elsewhere. You need to run the numbers for each of your options and can mix and match to get the best deal.

- You may get an even better deal by foregoing your employer's plan and buying health insurance on your own, or staying on your employer's plan yourself but having your spouse and kids sign up for their own policy. If they're healthy and live in a state with a competitive health insurance marketplace, they could reduce their premiums significantly.

- Don't automatically keep COBRA health insurance coverage with your former employer after you leave your job or get divorced. If you're healthy, you could find a better deal on your own.

- Raising your deductible to at least $1,050 for singles and $2,100 for family policies can save you a lot of money and help you qualify for a health savings account, which provides big tax benefits. The money you contribute lowers your taxable income, grows tax-deferred, and can be used tax-free for medical expenses at any age. Unlike flexible-spending accounts, which your employer may already offer, you don't have to use up the money by the end of the year.

- Maximize the tax benefits of your health savings account by not using the money for your current medical expenses. If you can afford it, pay your medical bills with other cash and leave the HSA money in the account to grow tax-deferred (or tax-free if used for healthcare costs). Shop for an HSA with low fees and good long-term investing options.

- Because higher deductibles and copayments mean you'll be paying a larger portion of your healthcare costs yourself, you need to become a smart healthcare shopper. Ask your doctor or pharmacist if you can switch to any lower-cost medications, shop for basic medical supplies on your own, make the most of free preventive care, and take advantage of your employer's tools to help minimize costs.

■ If you don't have health insurance through an employer, buying an individual policy may cost a lot less than you'd expect, especially if you're healthy and live in a state with a competitive health insurance marketplace. Shop around online and through an agent, comparing premiums as well as overall costs, and raise your deductible to qualify for an HSA.

■ Recent graduates who are healthy can generally get a much better deal by buying their own health insurance policy, keeping the deductible high, and qualifying for a health savings account, which can help them build a giant tax-free fund for future medical expenses. A short-term policy may be a cost-effective way to find coverage for just a few months. All of these options tend to be less expensive than staying on their parents' policy through COBRA, unless they're in poor health.

■ Health insurance prices vary a lot from company to company, especially if you have any medical problems. One insurer may reject you while another offers a great rate. It helps to work with an agent or broker who knows which insurers tend to be most competitive for people with your condition and the best strategies for strengthening your case. Shop around again if your health improves.

CHAPTER 2

HEALTH INSURANCE FOR RETIREES

■ ■ ■

Shopping for health insurance becomes totally different after age 65. Many people who retire early, work for themselves, or don't have jobs with health insurance spend their time counting down the days until they reach that magic age. At that point, you'll finally qualify for Medicare and get affordable coverage regardless of your medical condition.

That doesn't mean that once you reach 65 you can stop thinking about your health insurance. Medicare only covers slightly more than half of the average retiree's medical expenses, leaving most seniors to pay thousands of dollars every year in Medicare premiums, copayments, deductibles, and medical costs that the program does not cover at all. In fact, a study by the Commonwealth Fund found that the average Medicare beneficiary spends 22 percent of their income on medical expenses—even though they're on the government program.

There's an entire business set up around filling the gaps in Medicare. The best way is generally with retiree health insurance (if you're lucky enough to still have that option) even though many employers have been cutting back on benefits and raising premiums. Everyone else can buy either a Medicare supplement policy or a Medicare Advantage plan (generally Medicare HMOs) to help cover the bills. Even though the government has attempted to make it easier to shop for supplementary coverage, people still tend to make huge mistakes when picking a policy.

Most important, everyone needs to review their strategies for filling Medicare's gaps this year, even if they've been on the program for a long time. The Medicare Modernization Act of 2003 approved some of the most significant changes in the history of the government program. The new law filled one of Medicare's biggest gaps by creating Part D to provide prescription drug coverage. These new plans can save seniors a lot of money on their drug costs, but the government does not automatically enroll most people in the program. Instead, seniors generally need to pick a company and plan themselves and take the steps to sign up (some low-income seniors, however, are automatically enrolled). The program is complicated, the choices overwhelming, with more than 40 options in some parts of the country, and many Medicare beneficiaries haven't signed up because they're not sure whether the premiums are worth it. This can be a big mistake resulting in a loss of valuable coverage and a penalty to pay if they change their minds later. I'll discuss strategies for picking the right plan later in this chapter.

The new drug program is just one of many reasons why it's important to review your coverage right now. The new law also made other major changes in the way people 65 and older can pay for their healthcare services, introducing several new programs for filling other holes in Medicare, prohibiting some old strategies for supplementing the gaps, and giving private companies billions of dollars to improve their programs for Medicare beneficiaries. Some options that weren't always a good deal in the past, like Medicare HMOs, are now more prevalent and affordable. Other strategies that may have seemed acceptable a few years ago, like prescription drug coverage under a Medicare supplement plan, are now a horrible idea.

Because many of these changes also became effective on January 1, 2006, it's important for everyone to review all of their options now. If you have elderly parents and other relatives, help them, too. Many of the new choices are confusing—just think how complicated it can be to make these decisions if you are in poor health.

Medicare leaves some big gaps.

When you finally reach the age of 65, you'll qualify for Medicare and no longer need to worry about rejection by a health insurer or a huge surcharge because of your age or health. The government will pay for many of your medical bills and charges everyone the same amount, no matter how old or unhealthy you are. Medicare doesn't cover all of your medical expenses, though, and the coverage does cost some money, although admittedly a lot less than individual insurance. Medicare Part A (which covers hospital expenses) does not have a monthly premium if you or your spouse worked for ten years or more, but there's a $952 inpatient hospital deductible, a $238 daily coinsurance rate for days 61 to 90 in a hospital, and a $476 daily coinsurance for 60 lifetime reserve days in a hospital. There's also a daily coinsurance rate of $119 for days 21 to 100 of skilled nursing care (see Figure 2.1 on the next page).

Medicare Part B covers physician, lab, and other expenses, and has a monthly premium of $88.50 in 2006 ($1,062 per year), which is a 13 percent increase over the 2005 premium. It also has an annual deductible of $124 before coverage kicks in, and then leaves you with several other out-of-pocket costs. You pay 20 percent of the charge for doctor's visits (or more if your doctor doesn't accept Medicare's limits), and generally pay 20 percent of the Medicare-approved cost of diagnostic tests and x-rays, medical equipment, ambulance services, and other expenses. For a full list of what Medicare does and does not cover, see the government's Medicare Web site at *www.medicare.gov.*

Moreover, Medicare leaves two giant gaps: It's very difficult to qualify for Medicare coverage of nursing home expenses, which is why it's important to get long-term care insurance on your own (see Chapter 6). In addition, Medicare traditionally provided almost no coverage for prescription drugs. Starting in 2006, you can sign up for Medicare's new prescription drug plan, called Part D, but the average plan costs $32 per month ($384 per year) and leaves you

FIGURE 2.1 Medicare Costs in 2006

Your Share of Costs Under Medicare Part A

Inpatient Hospital Expenses
- $952 deductible per benefit period
- No coinsurance for days 1 through 60
- $238 daily coinsurance for days 61 to 90
- $476 daily coinsurance for 60 lifetime reserve days

Skilled Nursing Facility
- No deductible for each benefit period
- No coinsurance for days 1 through 20
- $119 daily coinsurance for days 21 through 100

Home Health Care
- No deductible or coinsurance
- Hospice care
- No deductible
- Small copayment for outpatient drugs and inpatient respite care

Your Share of Costs Under Medicare Part B

- $88.50 monthly premium
- $124 annual deductible
- 20 percent of doctor and other medical expenses of the Medicare-approved amount for providers who accept assignment (otherwise, the doctor can charge up to 15 percent above Medicare's approved amount)
- Nothing: Home healthcare and clinical diagnostic lab services
- 20 percent: Other diagnostic tests and x-rays, diabetes self-management supplies, durable medical equipment, physical therapy services, ambulance services, and chiropractor services
- 20 percent of blood after the first three pints per year
- 50 percent: Outpatient mental health services

---

with up to $3,600 in out-of-pocket costs before Medicare pays 95 percent of the bills. Private insurers are offering several variations on the plan, some charging a high premium in return for fewer out-of-pocket expenses and others are charging $20 or less per month for basic coverage.

You may need to buy several extra insurance policies to fill the gaps in Medicare, either through retiree health insurance, a Medicare Advantage plan (generally a Medicare HMO), or a Medicare supplement policy with a separate Part D policy for prescription drug coverage.

Retiree benefits are shrinking, but they may still be your best option.

As companies struggle to get their healthcare costs under control, they're taking the axe to retiree health insurance. In 1998, 66 percent of large companies (200 or more employees) offered retiree health insurance, according to the Kaiser Family Foundation. By 2005, that number had been cut in half, to 33 percent. Small companies are a lot less likely to provide retiree health benefits—just 7 percent of small firms offered the coverage—and these numbers are expected to shrink even further in the future. In a study by the Kaiser Family Foundation and Hewitt Associates, a human resources consulting firm, 11 percent of employers said they had eliminated subsidized health benefits for future retirees.

Meanwhile, the costs are increasing and the coverage shrinking for the few people who still have retiree health benefits. The typical worker under age 65 who retired in 2004 pays $2,244 annually in premiums ($4,644 with spousal coverage), which is 27 percent more than workers who retired in 2003. A typical Medicare-eligible worker who retired in 2004 pays $1,212 annually in premiums ($2,508 with spousal coverage), which is 24 percent more than workers who retired in 2003.

In addition to increasing premiums, many companies are increasing copayments for prescription drugs, raising deductibles and out-of-pocket spending caps for retirees, and a few eliminated their premium subsidy entirely—requiring retirees to pay 100 percent of the cost themselves.

Despite these cutbacks, retiree coverage still tends to be the best option because most employers continue to subsidize the bulk of the costs. In 2004, employers paid 61 percent of the average annual premium for new retirees over age 65, according to the Kaiser/Hewitt study. If your company raises rates and cuts back on coverage, it doesn't hurt to check your alternatives. You probably won't find a better deal anywhere else, and remember once you leave your employer's retiree health plan, you generally can't ever go back, but you should still explore your options.

Medigap can help, but some of the coverage isn't worth the money.

If you don't have retiree health insurance, a Medicare supplement policy (also called "medigap") gives you the most flexibility. The policy fills in many expenses that Medicare doesn't cover, and you can use any doctors or hospitals throughout the country.

The government attempted to make it easy to shop for medigap policies by creating 12 standardized policies, labeled A through L (Wisconsin, Minnesota, and Massachusetts have different plans). Every plan with the same letter has exactly the same coverage, no matter which insurance company offers it. Plan A has the least coverage and generally the lowest price tag; Plan J has the most comprehensive coverage but also costs the most. Plans K and L are new options that cover a portion of your costs, in return for a lower premium (see Figure 2.2).

To pick a plan, compare the extra premium to the dollar value of the additional benefits. Because Medicare covers a big part of your costs, there's generally a limit on the extra coverage you can get from the medigap policies. Sometimes the coverage is worth it, but some of the more expensive plans cost a lot in relation to limited extra coverage.

Plan A covers Medicare's $238 daily copayment for days 61 to 90 in a hospital, the $476 daily copayment for days 91 to 150, and payment in full for 365 additional hospital days during your lifetime. It also pays the 20 percent copayment for doctor's services and the cost of three pints of blood.

FIGURE 2.2 Medicare Costs in 2006

	A	B	C	D	E	F	G	H	I	J	K	L
Hospital Coinsurance Coinsurance for days 61-90 ($238) and days 91-150 ($476) in hospital; Payment in full for 365 additional lifetime days.	✓	✓	✓	✓	✓	✓	✓	✓	✓	✓	✓	✓
Part B Coinsurance Coinsurance for Part B services such as doctor's services, laboratory and x-ray services, durable medical equipment, and hospital outpatient services.	✓	✓	✓	✓	✓	✓	✓	✓	✓	✓	50%*	75%*
First three pints of blood	✓	✓	✓	✓	✓	✓	✓	✓	✓	✓	50%*	75%¹
Hospital Deductible Covers the first $952 of hospital charges for each benefit period.		✓	✓	✓	✓	✓	✓	✓	✓	✓	50%*	75%*
Skilled Nursing Facility (SNF) Daily Coinsurance Covers $119 per day for days 21 to 100 of skilled care in a nursing home per benefit period.			✓	✓	✓	✓	✓	✓	✓	✓	50%*	75%*
Part B Annual Deductible Pays the first $124 of covered physician and other Part B services per calendar year.		✓				✓				✓		
Part B Excess Charges Benefits 80% or 100% of Part B excess charges. (Under federal law, the excess limit is 15% more than Medicare's approved charge when provider does not take assignment; under New York State law the excess limit is 5% for most services.)						100%	80%		100%	100%		
Emergency Care Outside the U.S. Covers 80 percent of emergency care during the first two months of a trip after a $250 per calendar year deductible, up to a $50,000 lifetime maximum.			✓	✓	✓	✓	✓	✓	✓	✓		

FIGURE 2.2 Medicare Costs in 2006 (continued)

	A	B	C	D	E	F	G	H	I	J	K	L
At-Home Recovery Benefit Up to $40 each visit for custodial care after an illness, injury, or surgery, up to a maximum benefit of $1,600 a year.				✿			✿		✿	✿		
Preventive Medical Care Covers $120 per year for healthcare screenings ordered by a physician but not covered by Medicare, such as a physical examination, cholesterol test and diabetes screening. 100% coinsurance for Part B-covered preventive care services after the Part B deductible has been paid.	✿	✿	✿	✿	✿	✿	✿	✿	✿	✿	✿	✿
Hospice Care Coinsurance for respite care and other Part A-covered services.											50%*	75%*
Outpatient Prescription Drugs												
***Out-of-Pocket Maximum** Pays 100% of Part A and Part B coinsurance after annual maximum has been spent.											$4,000	$2,000

Medigap plans are standardized but each company sells the exact same plan for different prices. Shop around.

Source: Medicare Rights Center

All medigap plans cover these basic benefits, plus some additional coverage. Plan B, for example, adds the $952 inpatient hospital deductible before Medicare kicks in, but the cost can be steep in relation to the extra benefit, especially if you don't end up spending the full deductible. A 65-year-old woman would pay nearly $290 more each year for Part B than for Part A, on average, according to insurance-research firm Weiss Ratings.

Plan C includes the basic benefits and inpatient hospital deductible, plus several other benefits, including a skilled-nursing-facility benefit of $119 for each of days 21 to 100, the Medicare Part B deductible of $124 in 2006, and the cost of emergency care outside the United States (which will only be valuable if you travel abroad).

Plans D, E, and G don't cover the Part B deductible, but they have other coverage that can be of limited value, such as at-home recovery (which is difficult to qualify for) and preventive care (capped at just $120).

Most people choose Plan F, which has all of the benefits of Plan C (the second most popular) plus the difference between the doctor's bill and the amount allowed by Medicare (otherwise, doctors can charge up to 15 percent above Medicare's approved amount). If you go to doctors who don't accept Medicare's fees as payment in full, this extra coverage can be valuable, especially because the average Plan F actually costs less than Plan C, according to Weiss Ratings.

In some parts of the country, you can lower your premiums further by buying a high-deductible policy for Plan F, where you need to pay $1,730 in Medicare-eligible expenses before you can start to receive benefits. A 65-year-old woman in Florida could cut her premiums from about $1,800 to $1,000 by raising the deductible on Plan F. This strategy can save you a lot of money if you have few medical expenses and don't spend up to the full deductible anyway.

Plans H, I, and J provide limited prescription drug coverage, but insurers had to stop selling medigap policies with prescription drug coverage to new customers after the new Medicare prescription drug plan took effect on January 1, 2006. You can keep one of these policies if you already have it, but it's much better to switch to another medigap plan and get your prescription drug coverage through the Medicare program instead, which tends to have better coverage and a lower price tag (see more details below).

The new Medicare law also introduced plans K and L in 2006, which reduce some of the benefits in return for lower premiums. Most medigap plans cover 100 percent of the inpatient hospital deductible, the copayment for doctors' services, and a skilled-nursing-facility benefit. Plan K only pays 50 percent of those charges, with an annual out-of-pocket limit of $4,000, and Plan L pays 75 percent of those costs, with an out-of-pocket limit of $2,000. These policies can also be a better deal for people who are healthy and less likely to use the services anyway, but only if they save enough in premiums to make up for the extra expenses they may have to pay.

There are huge medigap price ranges for no good reason. You get absolutely nothing extra by going with a higher-priced policy.

Because every medigap plan with the same letter designation provides the exact same coverage, you'd think that prices would be similar from company to company. That's not the case. In fact, there are surprisingly huge price ranges for policies that provide identical coverage.

A 2005 survey by Weiss Ratings found that the price ranges for a 65-year-old woman buying Plan A vary enormously from company to company (see Figure 2.3). The lowest charged $355 per year while the highest charged $5,986. The price range was even bigger for Plan F, where the lowest-priced company charged $516 while the highest charged $10,789. Those figures are from a national survey, but the prices also vary within each state. In Florida, a 65-year-old woman can pay anywhere from $1,780 to $4,716 for Plan F.

You're getting absolutely nothing extra by going with the higher-priced policy. Because the plans are standardized, every Plan A has the exact same coverage; every Plan F has the exact same coverage—no matter which company you buy it from—and there's rarely any difference in customer service. Because the policies merely fill in the gaps left by Medicare, they'll have a tough time fighting you on claims; if Medicare approves the charge, they have to, too. Paying extra won't guarantee you a better company, either—some of the companies charging the highest rates actually have some of the worst financial-strength ratings.

FIGURE 2.3 Medigap Premium Rates in 2005

Plan	Minimum	Maximum	Average
A	$355	$5,986	$1,160
B	693	3,980	1,446
C	351	9,798	1,766
D	697	4,588	1,437
E	747	3,099	1,362
F	516	10,789	1,755

Calculations based on a 65-year-old female nationwide, excluding Minnesota, Wisconsin, and Massachusetts, which don't follow the standard A through J plan descriptions.
Source: Weiss Ratings

The only difference that you need to consider is how the company prices its policies. There are three types of pricing: issue age, attained age, and community rating.

- *Issue-age policies* base the price on your age when you buy the policy. If you buy the policy at age 65, for example, it's less expensive than if you buy it at age 70. However, your premiums won't increase just because you get older (although they can also rise because of healthcare inflation).
- *Attained-age policies* increase premiums as you get older, typically jumping every one, three, or five years (in addition to price increases due to healthcare inflation, which can happen to all medigap policies). To find out what has happened in the past, ask the company what it currently charges 70-, 75-, and 80-year-olds.
- *Community-rated policies* are similar to issue-age policies, but everyone in the same area pays the same price regardless of age (although some companies will offer up to a 20 percent discount for the first few years).

Attained-age policies may cost less in the beginning, but the price is more likely to increase through time. It's generally better to go with the lowest-cost issue-age or community-rated policy rather than worry about price increases with an attained-age policy. Interestingly, issue-age policies don't always cost more than attained-age policies anyway.

When shopping for a medigap plan first pick which letter plan will meet your needs the best, then go to your state insurance department to compare prices. Most state insurance department Web sites list prices for each insurer's medigap policies available in your area. See the National Association of Insurance Commissioners Web site (*www.naic.org/state_web_map.htm*) for links to your state regulator. You can also get a list of plans and prices available in your area through the Personal Plan Finder at *www.medicare.gov,* and you can find other good information about Medicare from the Medicare Rights Center Web site at *www.medicarerights.org.*

After you've narrowed down your list, check the insurer's financial strength rating. It can be worth a few extra dollars to go with a well-known company with good finances. You can see insurers' financial strength ratings, as well as a personalized list of medigap prices for someone your age in your area, by ordering Weiss Ratings Shoppers Guide to Medicare Supplement Insurance (cost $49; *www.weissratings.com* or 800-289-9222).

Medicare HMOs aren't as bad as they used to be.

Another way to fill in the gaps in Medicare is through a Medicare Advantage plan. Most of these plans provide your medical coverage through an HMO rather than through a combination of Medicare and a private medigap policy. They're a much better deal than they had been in the past. These plans were very popular throughout the mid-1990s as an inexpensive way to fill Medicare's gaps, especially if you were looking for affordable prescription drug coverage, as long as you didn't mind living in the world of managed care, which limits your list of doctors and has a gatekeeper control access to specialists.

These plans have changed a lot over the past ten years. Hundreds of companies left the business in the late 1990s, leaving seniors scrambling to find new coverage, and many doctors pulled out of the networks. From 1999 to the beginning of 2004, more than 2.4 million people with Medicare lost their HMO coverage, according to the Medicare Rights Center. The prices went up and the coverage went down for the remaining plans—especially prescription-drug coverage, which was significantly cut or even eliminated in many plans. In 1998, there were 346 Medicare Advantage plans throughout the country (then called Medicare+Choice). By 2004, that number had fallen to 154, and these plans weren't even available in many parts of the country. In 2004, only 62 percent of Medicare beneficiaries had a Medicare Advantage plan option in their area. The marketplace was clustered around a handful of states—at least 20 percent of the Medicare beneficiaries were enrolled in Arizona, California, Colorado, Oregon, Pennsylvania, and Rhode Island, with one in four Medicare Advantage enrollees in California.

That trend, however, is turning around. The Medicare Modernization Act of 2003, the same law that created the Medicare prescription drug program, gave Medicare Advantage plans a huge infusion of cash, increasing payments to the plans by $1.3 billion for 2004 and 2005. No surprise, more HMOs are starting to return to the marketplace. As a result, the number of plans increased by about 60 percent in 2005, as many plans expanded into parts of the country where they'd never done business before. Premiums dropped, too—some charge nothing in addition to the Medicare Part B premium ($88.50 per month in 2006), which had been common practice during the HMOs' heyday in the 1990s.

Another benefit of Medicare HMOs is their coverage for prescription drugs. Many have incorporated the new Medicare prescription drug program into their coverage at very low costs. If you don't mind managed care's control over your access to doctors, a Medicare Advantage plan can be an affordable way to pay for your care. First, run the numbers for your potential out-of-pocket costs for the year to make sure the policy will lower your total expenses, not just the premiums, and keep in mind that the HMO could end up boosting costs or leaving the business again if the government cuts its support. Also, find out about the plan's coverage when you travel—nonemergency care outside of the network generally isn't covered, so most snowbirds should pick a medigap policy instead.

Retirees can get big benefits from an HSA—another way to cover out-of-pocket costs.

You cannot contribute to a health savings account after you sign up for Medicare (age 65 for most people), but the money already in the account can give you a great stash to help pay costs that aren't covered by the government program. Even though you can use the money for nonmedical expenses after age 65 without a penalty, save it for medical expenses instead. That way, you'll also avoid the tax bill and stretch the money even further.

You can spend the HSA money on any qualified medical expense permitted under federal tax law and not covered by other insurance, including most medical care and dental and vision care, as well as prescription and over-the-counter drugs (such as aspirin).

You can also use the money to pay for Medicare premiums and out-of-pocket expenses including deductibles, copays, and coinsurance for Part A, B, C, or D. You cannot use the money for Medicare supplement insurance premiums, but you can use it tax-free to pay premiums for qualified long-term care policies. There's no time limit on using up the HSA money—and the longer you keep it in the account, the more you'll benefit from the tax-free growth.

Everyone should sign up for Medicare's prescription drug plan unless they already have better coverage—even if they have few drug expenses now.

Sweeping new laws took effect January 1, 2006, creating the biggest changes in Medicare's history since Lyndon Johnson first signed the program into law in 1965. For the past 40 years, Medicare provided very little coverage for prescription drugs. Now, the government program is offering prescription-drug coverage (called Part D), which you can buy through private companies. You are not automatically enrolled (unless you're below a certain income level), so you first need to decide whether or not to sign up, and then decide which insurer to buy it from and which variation of the plan to choose. People in many parts of the country have more than 40 different policy choices for stand-alone Part D policies, or they can get coverage for prescription drugs and other medical expenses through a Medicare Advantage plan. All plans have been approved by the government's Centers for Medicare and Medicaid Services.

There are many variations on the coverage, but under the standard plan, after you meet a $250 deductible, Medicare covers 75 percent of the next $2,000 of your drug costs. You pay the next $2,850 in drug costs yourself (what many people call the "doughnut hole") then Medicare pays up to 95 percent of your remaining drug costs (see Figure 2.4). The average premium for the standard plan is about $32 per month, although the coverage specifics and prices can vary

FIGURE 2.4 Standard Part D Coverage 2006

Total Drug Expenses	Part D Coverage	Out-of-Pocket Expense
$0–$250	$0	Up to the $250 deductible
$250–$2,250	75% of drug costs	25% of drug costs
$2,250–$5,100	$0 drug costs (doughnut hole)	100% of drug costs
$5,100+	95% of drug costs	5% of drug costs
		Total: $3,600 before catastrophic kicks in

a lot from company to company. Some plans are charging less than $20 per month, and other insurers fill in that doughnut hole in return for a higher premium.

Whether or not you should sign up depends on your current prescription-drug coverage.

If you have employee or retiree coverage, you should have received a notice from your employer explaining how your coverage compares with Medicare's plan. If the employer's plan is considered by actuaries to be equal or better to the plan offered by Medicare (called "creditable coverage" in government jargon), then it's generally best to stay with that plan. If the employer's coverage changes in the future and you decide to sign up for Medicare's plan later, you won't be hit with a penalty for late enrollment as long as your employer's plan had been considered to be "creditable coverage."

Employers received a government subsidy for keeping retirees in their own plans, so many will be offering "creditable coverage," which you should generally keep rather than signing up for Medicare's plan. Some employers, however, are pulling back on their prescription drug coverage and encouraging retirees to sign up for Medicare's plan instead. If you have retiree health insurance, it's essential to find out how the coverage compares to Medicare's program.

If you do not have any prescription drug coverage now, or if your employee or retiree coverage isn't as good as Medicare's, sign up for the government program as soon as possible—even if you have few drug expenses now. Otherwise, you won't have any coverage if you end up with big prescription bills in the middle of the year (you can generally only sign up for the plan from November 15 to December 31), and you'll be hit with a penalty if you change your mind later. If you're already 65 and enroll after May 15, 2006, you'll have to pay a penalty of 1 percent of the average national premium for every month you delay—a surcharge added to the cost of your Part D policy permanently. You won't have this penalty if you are already covered by a plan that is considered to be "creditable coverage." If you take few prescription drugs now, you can sign up for one of the low-cost Part D plans at first—some cost $20 per month or less—then change to one of the more-robust (and more expensive) plans if you end up taking more prescription drugs later on. You'll be able to change plans once a year, and your prescription needs are likely to increase every few years as you get older.

Ignore most of the calculators that claim to help you decide whether or not to sign up for the coverage, which are offered by insurers and consumer groups (and are very different from the essential calculator at Medicare.gov, which helps you choose a plan—see the next section for more details). These calculators generally take your annual drug costs and figure out how much money you'd save (or not) by signing up for Part D. However, these calculators tend to leave out a few key aspects to the Part D plans. They generally use the average premiums of $32, even though many plans charge less than that; they only use the standard Part D plan, even though insurers have introduced many variations in coverage; they assume all drugs will be covered equally (which usually isn't the case); and they don't take into consideration the penalty for late enrollment if you don't sign up for Part D right away.

Unless you already have better coverage, it's a good idea to sign up for Medicare prescription drug coverage even if you have few medical expenses now. Even if you buy a low-cost barebones plan now, you'll still have coverage for big expenses and you'll avoid the penalty for late enrollment. You can always switch to another plan during open enrollment season (November 15 to December 31) in future years.

Dump your medigap drug coverage. It was always a bad deal; now it's even worse.

When the new Medicare prescription drug law went into effect, private insurers had to stop selling new medigap prescription drug coverage (Plans H, I, and J) but could continue to offer the coverage to people who currently have it. However, if you do have a medigap drug plan, you should dump it and switch to Medicare's drug coverage instead. Because the Medicare coverage is subsidized by the government, it is a lot less expensive and provides more comprehensive coverage than the medigap prescription drug plans.

Plans H, I, and J, were never a very good deal—the limited coverage was rarely worth the extra premiums. Medigap Plans H and I only pay 50 percent of drug costs after a $250 deductible, up to a $1,250 annual benefit limit. Plan J raises the benefit limit to $3,000, but you only get that full amount if you have $6,250 or more in prescription costs. Medicare Part D, on the other hand, doesn't have a cap on the coverage amount—paying 95 percent of your drug costs after you pay $3,600 yourself—and providing more coverage at the lower levels, too. The price difference is huge: The average Medicare Part D plan costs $384 per year. The average medigap Plan H cost $3,229 in 2005. The medigap policies provide more than just prescription drug coverage, but Plan H still costs $1,474 more than the average Plan F, a similar policy without the drug coverage.

You still need a medigap policy to fill in Medicare's other holes, so it's a good idea to switch to another medigap plan (like Plan F) and buy a stand-alone Part D plan to cover your drug costs. Another alternative is to switch out of medigap entirely and get a Medicare Advantage plan that covers both drugs and other medical expenses. Medigap prescription drug coverage is not considered creditable coverage, so you'll need to make the move soon. Otherwise, if you eventually do want to sign up for Medicare's drug benefits, you'll end up paying the penalty of 1 percent of the average premium cost for every month you delay.

You can't just compare premiums when selecting a Medicare prescription drug plan.

Deciding whether or not you should get Medicare prescription drug coverage is only the first step. The other big decision is which policy to buy. That can be incredibly complicated. In some parts of the country, more than 20 insurers are selling the plans, and many of them are each offering two or three variations in coverage. In New York, for example, 21 insurers are offering a total of 46 plans. Some offer barebones coverage at a low premium, sometimes less than $20 per month. Some fill in the gaps in the standard coverage—like the deductible and doughnut hole—in return for a higher premium. Many charge different copayment amounts for different drugs, often with three pricing tiers based on the type of medications (with the lowest copayments for generic drugs).

For example, Humana offers three types of Part D plans. Its basic plan is the same as the Part D standard coverage—with the $250 deductible, then the plan covers 75 percent of the next $2,000 of your drug costs, then you pay the next $2,850 in drug costs yourself (the doughnut hole), and then the plan pays 95 percent of your remaining expenses. Premiums, which are based on regional medical costs, range form $1.87 to $17.91 per month.

Humana's enhanced plan, which costs between $4.91 and $25.36 per month, depending on your location, replaces the $250 deductible with a fixed schedule of copayments. You pay nothing for generic drugs, $30 for a one-month supply of each drug on the company's preferred list, $60 for a nonpreferred drug, and 25 percent of the cost of a specialty drug, until the total drug costs reach $250. Copayments are the same for the next $2,000 in drug expenses (with the exception of $7 for generics). After that, coverage is the same as the standard plan, so you have to pay the next $2,850 yourself.

On the high end, Humana's "complete" plan costs $38.70 to $73.17 per month and closes the doughnut hole, with the same copayments as the enhanced plan. Once your total out-of-pocket costs reach $3,600, the plan pays 95 percent of your annual drug costs.

A Florida resident, for example, would pay $10.35 per month in premiums for Humana's standard plan, $20.12 for the enhanced plan, and $61.70 for the complete plan. That means it would cost almost $500 extra per year to fill in coverage for the doughnut hole.

Sound confusing? Those are just three of more than 20 choices that many people have. Because each company has different premiums, copay amounts, and drug discounts, you need to run the numbers for your specific medications and compare total out-of-pocket costs for several plans. The good news: You only need to think about your expected drug costs for the upcoming year; you can always change plans during open enrollment period in the future.

If you have few drug costs now, focus your search on the companies' basic plans, which keep your premiums low but still provide coverage and help you avoid the penalty. If you take more medications, run your numbers through the plan compare tool at the Medicare Web site (*www.medicare.gov*) or call 800-633-4227 for personalized assistance. This calculator is very different from some insurers' and consumer groups' calculators, which do not do the calculations based on specific plans or drugs.

This Web tool makes shopping a lot easier—thank goodness, because it would be very complicated to compare plans otherwise. Type in the information about where you live, what drugs you take and dosages, and the calculator does the math for you, listing your total annual cost (premiums as well as copays for your specific drugs) for the plans available in your area. The tool also recommends ways to lower your costs by using generic alternatives.

After you've narrowed your options to a few good prospects, then compare three or four plans for details other than costs. Does your pharmacy participate in the plan? If you travel frequently, will your coverage go with you? Is there a discount for mail-order drugs? Check the insurance-company Web sites for more details about their plans, including calculators and lists of drugs and their costs.

If you do not have Web access, or if you want personalized attention, call the Medicare information number (800-Medicare) for information about your State Health Insurance Assistance Program, which helps seniors with their medical coverage questions. You can also check *www.healthassistancepartnership.org/program-locator/* for a list of local Medicare-related resources for seniors. The Medicare Rights Center (*www.medicarerights.org*) and AARP's Medicare Web page (*www.aarp.org/health/medicare*) also have a lot of helpful information about choosing a drug plan.

It's also a good time to review your prescriptions in general. Have your doctor or pharmacist review all of your prescriptions to see if you can switch to any lower-cost drugs, find out whether you have any duplicate coverage you can drop, and ask about any other strategies for lowering your expenses. You can find other ways to lower your drug costs through BenefitsCheckup (*www.benefitscheckup.com*), a resource tool created by the National Council on the Aging.

Low-income people may get free prescription drug coverage—if they know to sign up.

Medicare beneficiaries who currently get their prescription drug coverage through Medicaid (the government program for low-income people) are automatically enrolled in a Medicare Part D plan. These people (called "dual eligibles") do not pay the Part D premium or deductible and only pay $1 to $2 for generic drugs and $3 to $5 for brand-name drugs, until the total cost of their drugs (their share plus Medicare's share) reaches $5,100. At that point, they have no out-of-pocket expenses.

Many other low-income seniors can also get help paying for the Part D coverage, but only if they know how to sign up. If your savings, investments, and real estate (other than your home) is worth less than $11,500 if you're single, or $23,000 if married and living with your spouse, then you may qualify for a government subsidy to help cover the premiums and copayments for Part D—an average of $2,100 in extra help. Most people who are not on Medicaid need to apply for the subsidy through the Social Security Administration. For more information, call the Social Security Administration at 800-772-1213 or visit their Web site at *www.socialsecurity.gov/prescriptionhelp*. The Access to Benefits Coalition Web site (*www.accesstobenefits.org*) also has a lot of helpful information about the low-income subsidy and other help paying for prescription drugs.

TIPS FOR GETTING THE RIGHT COVERAGE AT THE BEST PRICE

After you turn age 65, the strategies for dealing with your health insurance are totally different than they were before you qualified for Medicare. Even though the government pays many of your medical bills from that point on, you still need to cover a lot of the costs yourself. You can buy several types of insurance to help fill in those gaps. Here are some strategies to help you pick the right plan and pay the best price:

- Retiree benefits are generally your best option, if you're still lucky enough to have coverage from your former employer.
- A Medicare supplement policy can fill in many of the gaps if you don't have good retiree coverage. When picking a plan, assess how much extra coverage you're getting for the additional cost. Most people choose Plan F or C.
- There are huge medigap price ranges for no good reason. Every policy with the same letter designation provides the exact same coverage, and customer service rarely varies. It's generally best to buy the lowest-priced policy for the letter designation you choose, but you need to know how the insurer sets its prices. Focus on companies with issue-age or

community-rated premiums, which do not rise just because you get older and tend to be lower over the long run than attained-age policies, which can raise your rate based on your age.

- Give Medicare HMOs a second look. After a big infusion of cash from the government, many Medicare Advantage plans are offering very low premiums for prescription drug and healthcare coverage, expanding to more parts of the country and returning to cities they left in the late 1990s.

- Everyone should sign up for Medicare's prescription drug plan unless they already have better coverage (such as through a former employer), regardless of their current prescription drug costs. Otherwise, you'll get stuck with a penalty of 1 percent of the national premium for every month you delay past May 15, 2006.

- You cannot just compare premiums when selecting a Medicare prescription drug plan. You need to look at overall costs—premiums as well as your out-of-pocket expenses under the plan for the particular drugs you take. The government's online calculator at *www.medicare.gov* is the best way to search for the plan that will cost you the least throughout the year.

CHAPTER 3

HOMEOWNERS INSURANCE

■ ■ ■

Most people spent little time thinking about homeowners insurance until recently. Because premiums are much lower than they are for health and auto insurance—less than $700 per year, on average—they tend to get a policy when they buy their homes, then make few changes through the years. That can be a very expensive mistake.

The importance of having the right homeowners insurance coverage became painfully obvious after four hurricanes battered Florida in 2004 and Katrina destroyed the Gulf Coast in 2005—the costliest catastrophe in American history. People who skimped on coverage to save a few hundred dollars ended up with tens of thousands of dollars in damages that insurance didn't cover. Many fought with their insurance companies over their claims for months, while neighbors who chose insurers with better customer service records started rebuilding soon after the disaster. Some who thought they had good insurance suffered from hundreds of thousands of dollars in uninsured losses because they hadn't updated their coverage through the years or hadn't bought the right types of insurance. Making small errors in your homeowners insurance can cause giant financial problems.

Even before the storms, insurers were already making it more difficult to get and keep your coverage. After suffering from financial troubles in the early 2000s, homeowners insurance companies started raising rates at a double-digit pace, dropping customers because they made just a few small claims, even if they were legitimately covered under their policies, and leaving some parts of the country entirely. They started relying more heavily on a semisecret claims database that makes it tough to find any insurer to cover you in the future—and can even make it difficult to sell your home. Insurance regulators received a record number of complaints from people who made just two or three claims for a few hundred dollars within a few years, then were dropped by their insurance company and ended up having to pay three times the premium with a new insurer, costing them much more in extra premiums than they ever received for the claims. That all started before the two costliest years for insurers in history—with seven out of the ten most-expensive hurricanes occurring between August 2004 and October 2005, and damages surpassing $83 billion over that time period.

Because of these changes, the rules for dealing with your homeowners insurance are totally different than they were just a few years ago. It's no longer safe to file small claims just because they're covered under your policy, switch to a lower-cost insurer just to save a few dollars, or skimp on coverage and expect your insurance company to make up the difference. You need to be much more careful to protect your coverage these days, and there's a lot at stake. After a surge in home prices, a larger percentage of most people's net worth is tied up in their homes. A huge part of your savings could be in jeopardy if your insurer won't pay to rebuild your home.

Here's how to make sure you have the right coverage, avoid big bills for uncovered losses, and protect yourself from getting dumped by your insurance company.

Don't file small claims—they could end up costing a lot more in extra premiums.

You'd think that when you buy homeowners insurance, you could submit claims for any damages covered under your policy. After all, that is the point of having insurance, right?

Not anymore.

Even though insurers must pay claims that are covered by your policy, the small claims could end up costing you a lot more money over the long run. At the least, you could lose a claim-free discount. Even worse, your insurer could drop you and make it tough to buy an affordable policy anywhere. Making a claim for a few hundred dollars could end up costing you thousands of dollars in extra premiums.

Most insurers offer claim-free discounts, generally shaving about 5 percent off your premium for every year you've gone without a claim, with a maximum claim-free discount of 25 to 35 percent after seven to ten years without a claim. If you pay $1,000 per year in premiums, for example, submitting a claim for $300 could actually end up costing you more in premium increases for the lost claims-free discount than you received from the insurance company to pay for the claim—and that's just in one year.

Even worse than that, submitting a few small claims could get you dropped the next time your policy is up for renewal. That's because insurance companies have been looking for any opportunity to improve their financial situations over the past few years. Paying small claims became very expensive, so they started dropping customers who were frequent claims filers. They're afraid that those people will be more likely to continue filing claims in the future, and are particularly worried about any claims for water-related damage, which could eventually lead to very expensive mold issues. In a study by the California Insurance Department, 25 percent of the companies refused to renew the policies of customers who made one or two nonwater damage claims in the past three years. And 32 percent refused to renew policies for people who made one or two water loss claims in the past three years.

The size of the claim doesn't matter—two claims for just a few hundred dollars can get you dropped. In one of many stories publicized by California Insurance Commissioner John Garamendi, who criticized insurers for this "use it and lose it" practice, a San Francisco woman filed a small claim when a car backed into an iron gate in front of her house, then another claim the next year when a neigh-bor's shingles fell into her gutter and caused water damage. One of the claims was for $600—just $100 more than her deductible. Her insurer ended up dropping her at the end of the policy term.

Getting dropped by even one insurer can be very expensive. Insurance companies share information with each other through a giant database called the Comprehensive Loss Underwriting Exchange (CLUE). After one company drops you, the others look at your CLUE record and are less likely to offer you coverage if you've filed some claims over the past few years. In the California Insurance Department study, 62 percent of the top 13 companies refused appli-cants with only one or two claims in the past three years.

The San Francisco woman who was dropped after making the two small claims had a tough time finding a policy elsewhere, and ended up having to pay $2,200 per year for coverage, three times the cost before she was dropped. In the end, making two claims for a few hundred dollars cost her nearly $1,500 in extra premiums ever year.

Before contacting your insurer about any small claim—even just with questions about it (some insurers count claims inquiries as claims on their customers' records)—first get estimates to see how much it will cost to fix the damages. Avoid submitting a claim if the damages cost less than $1,000 to repair, or if the repairs would be just a few hundred dollars more than your deductible. In addition, think carefully before buying coverage on valuables (like jewelry) that is worth less than $1,000. In most cases, coverage on valuables has a $0 deductible, which encourages you to make small claims that could also get you dropped.

Everyone should raise their deductible to at least $1,000. You will save money in premiums and be less likely to get dropped.

Raising your deductible to at least $1,000 can save you money in several ways. If it isn't safe to submit small claims for fear of your insurer dropping you, then you might as well get some benefit from it and not pay for coverage you aren't using anyway.

Increasing your deductible from $250 to $1,000 can lower your premium by as much as 25 percent. Going from $250 to $2,500 could cut your premiums by up to 30 percent. You'll save money in premiums, and you'll be a lot less likely to submit small claims, which could cost you a claims-free discount or get you dumped by your insurer. Then you can use the money you save to boost your coverage by tens of thousands of dollars. Raising your deductible from $250 to $1,000, for example, can generally give you enough in premium savings to buy an extra $50,000 in total coverage, which is very important because many people are underinsured. You'll only expose yourself to an extra $750 in out-of-pocket costs, but get $50,000 extra in insurance.

If you do raise your deductible by a few hundred dollars, make sure you keep enough money in your emergency fund to cover potential out-of-pocket costs. Keep the money safe in a money-market fund or money-market account, which you can access quickly in an emergency. Go to BankRate.com (*www.bankrate.com*) for the best money-market account rates or iMoneyNet (*www.imoneynet.com*) for the best money-market fund rates.

Get a CLUE—check the secret database where your claims can go to haunt you.

Your CLUE report includes information about the insurance claims you've made within the past five years, and claims made on your home even before you bought it. The problem with CLUE reports, though, is that they aren't always accurate. Sometimes just calling the insurer with questions about a claim ends up showing up as a full-fledged claim. In addition, just like with credit reports, it isn't unusual for someone else's information to show up accidentally on your report. Because so much is at stake, it's essential to make sure that the information about you is accurate.

It's easy to check your CLUE report. You can order it online from ChoiceTrust (*www.choicetrust.com*) or by calling 866-312-8076, a division of the company that maintains the database. Under the new rules of the Fair Credit Reporting Act, you can order one free copy every 12 months.

The CLUE report will show you the five-year history of losses for your name and your property, including the date and type of loss and the amount paid and the insurance company. The ChoiceTrust Web site also explains what to do if you dispute any information in the report.

A bad claims record can make it difficult to sell your home.

The homeowners insurance situation has gotten so tough that your house's claims history can make it difficult to get coverage—even if you didn't live there when the claims were made. Not only can this make owning a claim-heavy home expensive for the new buyers, who get stuck with high premiums, but also an active claims history can jeopardize the whole deal if insurers reject the application, because you'll generally need homeowners insurance before you can take out a mortgage.

Check out a house's insurance record before you make an offer to buy. The results could make a huge difference in prices—and the ability to get insured at all—in the future. Ask about previous claims, damages, and repairs, and review the house's CLUE report. Only homeowners and insurance agents can order a report, so you'll need to ask the seller or your agent for a copy. They can order a Home Seller's Disclosure Report for $19.50 from ChoiceTrust (*www.choicetrust.com*). This version of the CLUE report doesn't include personal information such as the homeowner's name, Social

Security number, and date of birth, and only lists information for that address—not any of the homeowner's previous addresses.

Then, search for a policy as soon as possible after you sign the contract on the house, rather than waiting until closer to closing, so you'll have extra time to shop around in case you get rejected by a few insurance companies at first. That's also a good idea because insurers in many states can cancel a policy within the first 60 days for any reason, and some do so after finding problems on the home's CLUE report.

If you're selling a home, check the CLUE report for any errors before you put the house on the market, so the buyer doesn't have an unnecessarily tough time getting coverage that could jeopardize the deal. Make good repairs and keep receipts in case the buyer's insurance company wants proof that any damages have been fixed.

Shopping around can save you big money, but don't switch companies just to save a few dollars.

The price of homeowners insurance can vary by hundreds of dollars from company to company. Insurers assess each risk separately, basing your premiums on the age of your home, the materials, its claims history, location, their profitability, and a slew of other factors. If they've paid out a lot of claims for similar houses in your area, they may charge you a lot more than another insurer who hasn't had to pay many claims for houses like yours.

You can get price quotes online at InsWeb (*www.insweb.com*) or through an independent agent who works with several companies. You can find a local independent agent at the Independent Insurance Agents & Brokers of America Web site (*www.iiaa.org*). Independent agents can be particularly helpful in high-risk areas where few insurers do business—they generally work with several companies and know from experience which are taking on new business, which are more likely to offer a good deal for your property, and which have a good customer service record at claim time.

A few major companies, such as State Farm and Allstate, only sell through their own agents and don't work with independent agents. You can find an agent in your area at *www.statefarm.com* or *www.allstate.com.*

Also be sure to get prices from the company that insures your car. Having both policies with the same insurer can save you up to 15 percent on both your homeowners and auto insurance premiums.

However, don't move away from a long-time insurer just to save a few dollars. You'll lose any claims-free discount you've built up, plus any additional premium savings you would have accumulated over the next few years because most of those discounts increase every year that you go without a claim. Moreover, your current insurer is generally less likely to drop you for making a small claim if you've been a long time-customer. During this tough time in the homeowners insurance business, protecting your current coverage can be more important than saving a few dollars in premiums.

When you do compare prices, beware of big differences in coverage. Get price quotes for the same insurance amount and deductible size, and make sure both insurers are providing the same type of payouts. Some policies will pay the replacement cost for your possessions—the cost to buy similar items now, no matter how long ago you originally bought them—but some offer "actual cash value," which subtracts depreciation from the payout amount. If you've owned the couch for ten years, for example, it will pay for the cost of a ten-year-old used couch today—not a new one. The replacement coverage is a lot more valuable and the difference in payout can be huge.

Saving some money in premiums can backfire if your insurer hassles you about paying claims.

Homeowners insurance claims are some of the most complex to settle, with the potential for hundreds of thousands of dollars in payout differences based on the way the company does business. In addition, the time it takes to get a claim paid can vary enormously from company to company, especially after a major disaster.

Six weeks after Hurricane Katrina, for example, many policy-holders struggled to contact their insurance companies and still hadn't seen an adjuster. After they finally got an appointment, they had to provide detailed records about every item that was damaged, then waited several more weeks until the claim money started to trickle in. Some had to fight with their insurers about what was covered and what wasn't, with final claim settlement dragging out for months. On the other hand, other insurers used satellite imagery to check out damages and immediately paid claims. Those policyhold-ers could hire scarce contractors quickly while their neighbors con-tinued to live in rented apartments and waited for their checks to arrive.

The differences in customer service were also obvious after the Florida hurricanes of 2004. Almost a year later, many houses were completely repaired while their neighbors' homes still had blue tarps covering their broken roofs and owners who were fighting with their insurance companies.

After you've narrowed down your list to a few companies, check out their complaint records. Saving a few dollars in premiums can backfire if the insurer is stingy at claim time. It's easy to look up a company's customer-service record before making any changes. Most state insurance department Web sites keep information about the companies' complaint records. You can find links to each state regulator's Web site at the National Association of Insurance Com-missioners Web site (*www.naic.org/state_web_map.htm*).

Focus on the complaint ratio (the number of complaints for every dollar the insurer collects in premiums), so large insurers aren't penalized just because they do more business. It's most important to check out the insurer's record in your own state, but it can also help to look up their complaint records in states that had big disasters, such as areas with frequent hurricanes, to see how the insurer stacks up under pressure. The insurance department Web sites also report actions taken against the insurance companies, such as fines for slow payouts or other problems handling claims.

You can also check the company's national claims-paying records by using the National Association of Insurance Commissioners' Consumer Information Source (*www.naic.org/cis/index.do*). Type in the company name and click on "property/casualty" for the business type, which includes homeowners and auto insurance (there's a separate category for life/accident/health insurance). Click on "closed complaints" and then the "complaint ratio report" and "homeowners insurance." The site then shows the company's ratio on a helpful graph to illustrate how the insurer's complaint ratio compares to the national average. If the insurer's record is worse than average, you may want to search for another company—even if the premiums are a bit higher. Paying a few extra dollars for a company with a good track record can make a big difference if you ever have a claim.

Long-time independent insurance agents are also a good source of information about companies' claims-handling reputations. It hurts their business when customers leave after insurers hassle them about claims, so they generally try to work with companies that make their customers happy. Also talk to your neighbors about their experiences, especially if you live in a high-risk area, have had any disasters nearby over the past few years, or live in an older or unique house.

Don't take no for an answer. A few key strategies can help you get coverage, even if you've been rejected.

If your insurer sends you that dreaded letter refusing to renew your homeowners policy, there are plenty of ways to fight back.

First, call the company or your agent and ask if there's anything you can do to reverse the decision. Sometimes raising your deductible helps because the insurer is less likely to get stuck paying out small claims. Instead of raising it just to $1,000 or $2,500, some are asking for your deductible to equal a percentage of your home's value, asking for a 2 percent deductible, for example, before they'll pay out. That can still be valuable. Even if you have to pay $4,000 on a $200,000 house, you'll still have important coverage for major damages.

If one part of your home seems particularly risky, like an old boiler, find out if replacing it can help you keep the coverage. If you've made several water-damage claims, offer to get a new roof or fix any other big damages that could eliminate related claims in the future.

If the insurer is trying to pull out of your area, which many are doing in the hurricane-prone southeast, it may be more likely to take you on as a new customer if you have both your car and home insured with the same company.

Also shop around. Each insurance company has different rules for rejecting and accepting customers, based on its own research and claims experience. One may turn you down while another offers you a great rate. That's where it can really help to work with an independent insurance agent, who knows from experience which companies are more likely to offer a better deal to homes like yours.

If you do get rejected by several companies, you may need to resort to the insurance pool. In 32 states, homeowners who can't get coverage elsewhere can get insurance from their state's high-risk pool, often called a FAIR plan (Fair Access to Insurance Requirements). The deductibles are generally high—often 2 percent to 5 percent of the insured amount—and some cap coverage amounts at just $100,000. Others exclude some coverage that comes with standard homeowners insurance, not covering personal liability or windstorms, for example. This may be your only option, however, and it's a lot better than going without coverage, even if your mortgage company doesn't require it. Check out several other insurers first—both on your own and through an independent agent—just in case you can find a better deal somewhere.

Your dog may cost you your insurance.

Homeowners insurance typically covers dog-bite liability—up to the policy's liability limits (typically $300,000 to $500,000)—and insurers have been making huge payouts in dog-related cases. In 2003, dog bites accounted for about one quarter of all homeowners insurance liability claims, costing about $322 million, according to the Insurance Information Institute. That's actually a slight decrease from nearly $346 million of dog-bite claims from the previous year, in part because insurance companies started cracking down on their dog-bite liability. In some cases, you may now have a tough time finding insurance if your dog is considered to be an aggressive breed by insurers, such as pit bulls and rottweilers, and sometimes Doberman pinschers, Akitas, and chow chows—even if they've never bit anyone.

The rules vary from company to company. Some insurers will cover these dogs without a problem, others will automatically deny them, and some may require you to buy a separate liability policy to cover any injuries caused by these types of dogs, or raise your rate because of your dog's breed.

If the dog bites anyone, some insurers will refuse to renew your policy, or will boost your premium or exclude the dog from coverage (forcing you to pay for any dog-related lawsuits). Any dog-bite claims will appear on your CLUE report and can make it very difficult to find a policy with another company. Some companies won't insure you for three years after having a dog-bite claim, even if you no longer own the dog. A few provide a 10 percent discount if you take the dog off the policy, which usually isn't a smart move because you could be on the hook for large legal bills if anything happens (and could make the 10 percent discount look tiny in comparison).

Because the rules vary so much by company, it's important to shop around, especially if your insurer is charging you a higher rate for a dog that has never bitten anyone (or if you have a dog that has bitten and are struggling to find new coverage). Go to *www.iiaa.org* to find an independent agent in your area or contact other agents and ask specifically about their companies' policies towards canceling or refusing to renew a policy based on your dog. Your dog's national breed club may also have ideas because many of their members have personal experience in trying to find a good policy. You can find links to your national breed club at the American Kennel Club's Web site (*www.akc.org*).

The rules can also vary by state. Some states, like Michigan, now only let insurers drop someone because of a dog's bite history, but won't allow them to drop a customer just because they own a particular breed of dog. For more information about state laws and other tips for finding homeowners insurance, see the American Kennel Club's insurance resource center (*www.akc.org/insurance/homeowners_inscenter.cfm*).

If you have trouble getting coverage, it can help to show the insurer that your dog has completed an obedience training program, such as the AKC's Canine Good Citizen Program, which is a ten-step certification program focusing on good manners for dogs.

GETTING THE RIGHT COVERAGE

Getting a good deal on your homeowners insurance is only part of the job. It's even more important to make sure you have the right coverage. Many people are underinsured or don't have the right types of coverage, which can devastate their financial plans.

You're probably underinsured—and rising home prices have nothing to do with it.

Residents of the Gulf Coast faced another disaster months after Hurricane Katrina hit, when many discovered that they had way too little insurance coverage. After they finally tracked down contractors to fix the damage, they found out that their insurance payouts were

going to fall tens of thousands—sometimes hundreds of thousands—
of dollars short of the amount needed to rebuild their homes.

This should not have come as a huge surprise. Marshall & Swift/
Boeckh (MS/B), which provides rebuilding cost estimates to insurers, believes that nearly 700,000 of the 1.18 million homes in Louisiana were underinsured, and the underinsurance problem is
universal. Marshall & Swift/Boeckh says that 59 percent of American homes are underinsured by an average of 22 percent—that's not
even counting the extra cost of bulldozing a totally destroyed home
and tracking down scarce material and contractors after a major
disaster.

People had similar problems after Southern California's wild-
fires in 2003. More than 2,700 people filed total-loss claims with
their insurance companies, and about 22 percent of them complained
to the California Department of Insurance about the way their claims
were handled. Half of those complaints were about underinsurance.

So many people were caught off guard because many insurers
had just made big changes to the amount of coverage they provide.
Until a few years ago, most insurance companies would provide
"guaranteed replacement cost," paying whatever it took to rebuild
your home, even if it cost a lot more than the coverage amount you
bought. After losing a lot of money, though, most insurance companies started to cap payouts at 120 percent of the coverage amount
purchased—paying up to $300,000, for example, if your home was
insured for $250,000. That provides some wiggle room for extra
costs after a major disaster, but shifts the burden to you to make sure
you have enough coverage.

Most people did have the right amount of insurance when they
bought their homes, but then didn't update their limits to keep up
with rising building costs or increase the amount of coverage when
they did major home improvements, added additions to their property, or made upgrades to their home (like installing high-end kitchen
appliances, hardwood floors, or a fancy bathroom) that cost a lot
more to replace.

Calculating the right insurance amount has nothing to do with the market value of your home, which includes both the building and the land. You don't need to buy insurance to cover the value of the land—even if your house is totally destroyed, the land is still there—but you need enough to pay to replace the building. If you own a simple tract home in a desirable neighborhood, your home's replacement cost may be a lot less than its market value, but if you own a historic home with a lot of unique architectural details and top-of-the-line appliances and materials, it might actually cost more to rebuild your home than you could buy it for today.

You can get a general idea of your home's replacement cost by asking a local builder about average building costs in your area and multiplying that number by the square footage of your home. That won't, however, take into consideration your home's special features. It's better to ask your insurance agent or company to reassess your home's replacement value every few years (more frequently when you do major home improvements) or hire an insurance appraiser. Another option: MS/B now has a tool available on the AccuCoverage Web site for $19.95, which lets consumers type in details about their homes and access the same building-cost estimates that insurers use.

Including an inflation protection provision in your policy can help, but it's still important to double check your insurance amount every few years because the cost of some types of materials have been rising at a much higher rate than inflation. It's also best when the inflation protection is tied to regional rather than national building costs because prices can vary a lot throughout the country.

Even if you have inflation protection, your insurance amount will not automatically adjust to cover any home improvements, so you'll have to notify your insurer to increase the coverage amount. Don't be afraid to make that call. The extra cost will be minimal and it's the only way to get the right amount of protection. It generally costs from $50 to $100 to increase your dwelling limits from $250,000 to $300,000. Increasing your deductible from $250 to $1,000 can easily pay for the extra coverage.

Another option: Pay extra for a company that offers extended replacement cost coverage. A few high-end insurers, like Chubb and Fireman's Fund, still sell policies that don't cap your coverage at 120 percent of the insured amount. You may pay extra for the policies, but you generally get a lot more coverage, including a promise that the insurer will pay the full cost to replace the house, even if it's a lot more than the amount of coverage you bought. It's up to the insurer to make sure the insurance amount is keeping up with actual rebuilding costs, so they'll generally send appraisers out to your home every few years.

All homeowners insurance policies have some huge gaps.

A huge problem after Hurricane Katrina was determining whether flooding or windstorm caused the damages, which can make a tremendous difference in the payout. Homeowners insurance covers wind-driven rain; generally water coming in through the windows, the roof, doors, or holes in the walls, but it doesn't cover flooding. After the storm, many insurers sent adjusters out to inspect each house and look for a water line that would prove the damage was caused by flooding. In that case, the homeowners insurance claim would be denied, leaving people with hundreds of thousands of dollars of damage that wasn't covered by insurance unless they had purchased a separate flood policy. Because many people—and their lawyers—claim that both the windstorm and the flood caused the damage and, therefore, should be covered, expect the battles about coverage to last a long time.

Flood coverage can also be valuable if you never get hit by a record-breaking hurricane. Even if water just seeps into your basement, the damages can still be expensive. You may need to replace carpeting, furniture, clothes, and sometimes even sheet rock and wall coverings because of the threat of mold. Moreover, you need to mitigate water damage right away, before the mold situation gets worse.

You can get flood insurance from the federal government's National Flood Insurance Program (*www.floodsmart.gov*). People living in flood-prone areas are generally required to buy flood coverage by their mortgage companies, but it's a good idea to buy the coverage even if you don't live in a high-risk flood area. Before Katrina, 25 percent of all flood-loss claims were filed in low-to-moderate risk areas, and even though many areas hit by Katrina were always considered risky, some had never flooded in the past and the homeowners weren't required to buy the coverage. Then they lost their homes after a 30-foot storm surge engulfed their cities. Don't wait to buy a policy until you hear that a storm is brewing; there's usually a 30-day waiting period before the policy takes effect.

If you're in a low-risk area, flood insurance can be quite inexpensive. You can buy $100,000 of coverage for your house and $40,000 for its contents with a $500 deductible for about $233 per year. In a high-risk area, coverage could cost $860 to almost $1,900 or more per year, depending on the location, elevation, construction, and other factors. Asses your risk and find names of agents who can sell the policies at *www.floodsmart.gov.* You may be able to buy a policy from your own homeowners insurance agent (many sell the government's policies), which may make your claim much less complicated. State Farm is one of a few private insurers that settle flood claims for the federal flood program, for example, and its customers generally had a much easier time getting their Katrina claims paid because they only had to deal with one company. State Farm used satellite imagery to assess flood damages immediately in some communities and quickly paid many flood claims.

In some cases, though, even maxing out the flood insurance isn't enough. The maximum you can buy is $250,000 in coverage for your home and $100,000 for its contents, and coverage is limited for art, collectibles, jewelry, and for many items in your basement. If that coverage amount is too little, then consider buying an excess flood policy. Some high-end companies, like Chubb and Firemen's Fund, sell excess flood policies to their customers (you must also have your homeowners insurance through them), which fill in the gaps, often with the same coverage levels as their homeowners insurance policies. Chubb's excess flood policy costs from eight cents to $1.89 per $100 of valuation, depending on the location and how well protected your home is.

Another big gap is earthquake coverage. The California Earthquake Authority provides earthquake coverage for Californians through private insurers. The standard CEA policy has a 15 percent deductible, and covers personal possessions only up to $5,000 and additional living expenses only up to $1,500. CEA also offers a more-expensive policy with a 10 percent deductible, insurance for other structures (like stand-alone garages and pools), personal items up to $25,000, and $10,000 loss of use coverage. Premiums vary within California's 19 rating territories based on type of house, age, nature of the soil, and proximity to fault lines. The average earthquake policy costs $500, but policies in riskier areas can top $3,000 per year. You can get more information at the California Earthquake Authority Web site found at *www.earthquakeauthority.com* or by calling 877-797-4300, but you can only purchase the policies through homeowners insurance companies that are members of the CEA. Ask your agent about coverage.

People in other parts of the country can generally get earthquake coverage as a rider added to their homeowners insurance, or a separate policy from private insurers. Prices vary significantly based on your region, the house's materials, and other risks. According to the Insurance Information Institute, earthquake insurance on a frame house in the Pacific Northwest might cost from $1 to $3 per $1,000 of coverage, but might cost less than 50 cents per $1,000 on the East Coast. A brick home in the Pacific Northwest would cost about $3 to $15 per $1,000 to insure; while costing 60 to 90 cents in New York.

You can't buy extra coverage for some risks—but you can boost your emergency fund.

Homeowners insurance generally does not cover some smaller items, and you may not be able to buy extra coverage to fill in those gaps, which can lead to big out-of-pocket expenses after a storm.

Insurers will generally cover damage to your house caused by fallen trees and about $500 for removal, but provide no coverage if the tree doesn't hit your home. It's easy to spend several thousand dollars to remove large trees that fall after a storm.

In addition, if you're raising your deductible to $1,000 or $2,500, be sure to keep that much money in a liquid account, so you don't have to go into debt or sell stocks to cover your costs. If you live in a high-risk area, your deductible may be even higher—people on the Florida coast routinely have to pay deductibles as high as 2 percent to 5 percent of their home's insured value (that's $6,000 to $15,000 on a house insured for $300,000)—or you may have a high deductible for windstorms and a lower one for other damages.

Keep the money in a safe and liquid account so you can cover those expenses quickly. For the best rates for money-market accounts, see *www.bankrate.com* and for money-market funds see *www.imoneynet.com*.

You probably have very little coverage on your valuables.

Homeowners insurance generally covers your possessions up to 50 percent of your dwelling coverage. That means if you have $300,000 in insurance to rebuild your home, your possessions will generally be covered up to $150,000. Most policies, however, have much lower limits on specific types of valuable items, typically paying only $1,000 to $1,500 for jewelry, $2,500 for firearms, $2,500 for silverware, and similar limits for artwork, collectibles, and musical instruments.

It's easy to get extra coverage to boost those limits. Buying a special rider to cover the specific items can provide you with more coverage—insuring it up to the appraised amount, without subtracting depreciation—and you'll have coverage for more situations. A jewelry rider will cover mysterious disappearance (paying out if you lose the ring), which may not be covered under a standard homeowners insurance policy.

A jewelry rider generally costs $15 per $1,000 of the jewelry's value, with discounts if you keep it in a vault. Extra coverage for antiques or artwork generally costs $2 to $3 per $1,000 of value, and coverage for silver and furs generally costs $5 per $1,000 of value.

Do not buy jewelry coverage, however, for items worth less than $1,000. The jewelry riders have a $0 deductible and may entice you to file a small claim, which could eventually get you dropped and make it tough to get insurance with another company, or at least cost you a claims-free discount. Instead, cover small losses yourself and buy the coverage for items worth more than $1,000.

Two little-known types of extra coverage can end up being very valuable.

As insurers were trying to pull back on their risk over the past few years, they not only cut down on guaranteed replacement cost coverage, but they also eliminated some other types of coverage that had automatically been included in their policies. Some of this coverage can be very valuable but now requires a special rider. The riders aren't very expensive, but you need to know to ask for them.

One surprisingly important rider provides sewage backup coverage. Sewage backup problems are some of the most disgusting problems that can plague a house—the sewage drains run backwards and the waste that was supposed to leave your home ends up coming back in. Removing raw sewage from your home can be quite expensive, often requiring removal of carpets, furniture, clothing, and anything else affected in order to eliminate the stench and the threat of mold. The bills can easily add up to thousands of dollars.

Sewage backup problems used to be covered automatically in most homeowners insurance policies, but now the coverage is generally excluded unless you buy a special rider. The rider costs about $50 per year for $10,000 of coverage. It's worth the extra money, especially if you have a finished basement with valuable furniture or equipment. Some insurers, however, no longer offer the rider at all or restrict coverage on electronics in the basement. Find out what the policy covers before comparing costs.

Another surprisingly valuable rider can provide "building and ordinance" coverage. Homeowners insurance policies generally pay to replace your home to the way it was before the damage, but the local building codes may have changed since your house was built, requiring new houses to meet higher standards for electrical wiring, plumbing, storm resistance, and other features. Rebuilding your home to its previous state may no longer be an option; and upgrading to the new codes can be a lot more expensive. Your homeowners insurance policy generally won't cover these extra costs, which can also add up to tens of thousands of dollars or even more in areas where the codes have changed significantly. A building and ordinance rider provides extra money to bring the home up to the new requirements.

This coverage is essential for people in Florida whose homes were built before Hurricane Andrew in 1992, and will probably be the case in the future for homes in southern Louisiana and Mississippi that made it through Hurricane Katrina. It can also be valuable for anyone with a historic home in a neighborhood where the rules have changed throughout the years.

The coverage tends to cost about $60 to $70 to increase your insurance amount by 50 percent to bring it up to new building codes.

Many people pass up free money from their insurer because they don't know to ask for it.

Policy discounts are like free money—cutting your premiums without sacrificing any coverage. However, many people give up potential discounts because they don't know to ask for them.

Ask your insurance company for a list of discounts, and let them know whenever you qualify (see Figure 3.1). Some insurers offer a 10 to 25 percent discount if you are 55 or older, retired, and living in your principal residence. Most cut your premiums on both your auto and homeowners insurance if you have both policies with the same insurer, and you can gradually accumulate a 25 to 35 percent discount after going for several years without filing a claim (one of the key reasons to increase your deductible to $1,000 and avoid submitting small claims). A few insurers also offer nonsmoking discounts, so it's important to let your insurance company know if you've quit.

A few investments can lower your premiums significantly, and the cost savings can eventually pay for your home improvements. You'll generally get 15 to 20 percent off your homeowners insurance premium for installing a home-security system, storm shutters, or using certain roofing materials. Adding smoke detectors, fire alarms, and deadbolts can also cut your costs.

Before you make any of these changes, find out what you need to do to get the discount. Insurers generally have very specific criteria about which items qualify and how they must be installed. Then tell your insurer that you've made the changes; otherwise, you won't get credit for making them.

You automatically lose a huge chunk of your coverage if you have a home office.

The minute you do business in your home, parts of your insurance coverage can drop by tens of thousands of dollars.

FIGURE 3.1 Homeowners Insurance Discounts

Homeowners insurance discounts vary from company to company and state to state, but ask your insurer if any of the following can help lower your price:

- Several years without filing a claim
- Homeowners and auto insurance with the same company
- Retirement
- Being a nonsmoker
- Home-security systems and deadbolt locks
- Storm shutters and other storm-resistant improvements
- Certain roofing materials
- Smoke detectors and fire alarms
- A home that is less than ten years old
- Jewelry kept in a vault

Homeowners insurance generally covers your possessions up to 50 percent of your dwelling coverage, covering up to $150,000 in possessions, for example, on a house insured for $300,000. However, the policies tend to have lower limits for things like jewelry, art, silver, guns, furs, and electronic equipment, and if you use any of that equipment for business the coverage tends to drop even lower—to just about $2,500. It could easily cost $10,000 or more to replace a home office with a computer, printer, fax machine, nice desk and fancy chair, phone system, laptop, and other basic office equipment, but the coverage on everything will drop to just $2,500 if the insurer finds out that the room was used for business. That low limit may even apply if you have a rider on your policy that increases the coverage for personal computers, if those computers were used for business. Even worse, most homeowners insurance policies cover just $250 of business property that is stolen and has to be replaced—nowhere near enough to cover your laptop.

One of the biggest risks comes from the shrinkage in your liability coverage when you use part of your home as an office. Even if you have $1 million in liability coverage on your homeowners insurance policy, that coverage amount will fall to $0 for liability related to your business if, for example, a delivery person slips and falls while delivering you a business package (this is different from mal-practice or errors and omissions insurance, which covers liability caused by something you do in your business and is separate cover-age required by doctors, architects, and other professions).

Your insurer may offer to double the coverage on business equip-ment in your home office for as little as $25 per year, but that may not be enough to replace your computer system, and still leaves you vulnerable with absolutely no coverage for any business-related lia-bility. A better strategy is to buy a business-in-home rider, which increases the coverage levels for your business property and liability to the same levels you have on the rest of your homeowners policy. This rider generally costs about $150 per year if you have a basic consultant's office with a computer system and don't have clients visiting your home. Higher-risk businesses may need a stand-alone businessowners' policy, which could cost $350 per year or more. A standard businessowners' policy may also cover the loss of equip-ment caused by power surges or loss of income if you cannot do your job because your equipment broke down or your office was destroyed by a storm, fire, or other covered event.

Business policies, however, don't cover two important risks; workers' compensation and business liability (errors and omissions or malpractice). If anyone works for you as an employee, your state may require you to provide workers' compensation insurance, which covers medical bills and lost wages for an employee hurt on the job. The cost is usually based on the size of your payroll, with minimum premiums of $250 to $500 per year. A business policy will cover lia-bility in the course of your business, such as if someone trips while delivering a package, but it won't cover liability caused by the result of your work if, for example, you're an architect who builds a home that collapses and hurts people. You'll need to buy a separate policy for that, which is generally a lot more expensive.

Renters insurance is cheap—and very valuable.

Even if you don't own your home, you can still own a lot of stuff. Your electronics, furniture, clothes, appliances, kitchenware, and everything else can easily add up to thousands of dollars. According to State Farm, the average person has more than $20,000 worth of stuff. If you rent an apartment, however, none of it would be covered by insurance unless you have a renters policy, and even though damages to the building will be insured by your landlord's policy, you won't have any liability coverage for yourself. If your child is away at college, your homeowners insurance policy may cover items in their dorm room, but might not provide any coverage if they live in an off-campus apartment.

Renters insurance is incredibly cheap, generally just $100 to $200 per year, and you may get a discount on both your renters and auto insurance if you buy both policies from the same company. Raising your deductible to $1,000 can cut your premiums even more.

To figure out how much you need, add up the value of all the items in your apartment. The Insurance Information Institute's "Know Your Stuff" home inventory software walks you through each room and makes it easy to add more information later. Then keep a copy of that inventory in a safe place away from your apartment, which will make it a lot easier to collect your money if you ever have a claim. It's also a good idea to get about $300,000 of liability coverage in the renters policy.

Low limits on liability coverage could expose you to the most expensive risks. An umbrella policy costs very little for a lot of coverage.

People generally think about buying homeowners insurance to pay for damaged property and cover rebuilding costs, but one of the most valuable parts of the insurance is the liability coverage. If someone hurts themselves at a party, if your dog bites a neighbor, or if a friend falls down your steps, your homeowners insurance generally provides about $300,000 of liability coverage to cover damages and legal fees if you are sued. You may be able to increase your coverage to $500,000 for about $25 more per year.

Even that, however, may not be enough to cover some large lawsuits—especially as the size of verdicts continues to increase. You could be sued for everything you're worth, plus future earnings. To protect that money, you can boost your coverage by $1 million by buying an umbrella policy, also called "excess liability coverage." These policies cover you for both auto and homeowners liability, and they only pay out after you've used all of the liability coverage on your home or auto policy. You generally need to keep the maximum liability coverage on your auto and homeowners insurance—often $500,000—before you can buy an umbrella policy.

It's important to get a liability policy if your home, investments, and assets plus future earnings are worth $1 million or more. The policy can be even more valuable if you entertain frequently, have a dog that could bite, own a boat or second home, a swimming pool, have a high public profile, or do anything else that exposes you to more risk.

Because these policies only cover very large lawsuits, the price is surprisingly small—about $250 to $350 per year for $1 million in coverage. The next $1 million generally costs about $75, and you may only pay about $50 for every million after that. You may also get a 15 percent discount on your umbrella, auto, and homeowners insurance policies if you buy all three types of coverage from the same insurer. Having all of the coverage together also makes it easier to settle claims.

Treat your inventory like cash.

It's much easier to make an inventory before the disaster, then give the list, photos, or videotape to the adjuster, rather than trying to

FIGURE 3.2 Dealing with Claims

The steps you take after a disaster occurs will affect how quickly—and how much—the insurer ends up paying you. Here's what you can do to make the claims process go as smoothly as possible:

- Insurers generally want you to take steps to prevent further damage after a major storm, like boarding broken windows and putting a tarp over a damaged roof, and they'll reimburse you for those expenses. They do not, however, want you to make repairs until you've met with an adjuster, which can take quite a long time after a major disaster. Six weeks after Hurricane Katrina, for example, many people were still waiting to meet with adjusters, who were swamped with hundreds of thousands of claims.
- Take before and after photos, and keep the receipt for the tarp and any other temporary fixes you've made. Talk with your claim representative before throwing away any damaged personal property.
- Most insurers will pay for "additional living expenses" while your house is uninhabitable, generally up to one or two years (the limits vary by company) of expenses beyond your normal living costs. Keep the receipts for temporary housing, meals, and other expenses.
- Try to catalog the damage. Having an inventory ready to go will make it a lot easier to get the full amount for your possessions. Insurers generally pay *up to* 50 percent of the dwelling value for your possessions, but that 50 percent is the maximum, and they'll only pay for what you had, so you'll need to provide as much evidence as possible in order to maximize your payout. Having a detailed inventory ahead of time will help your claim get settled faster and eliminate some controversies about what you owned and how much it was worth.
- When you're dealing with the insurance company and adjusters, keep records of everyone you've talked with and what they've said. If you end up having troubles getting the claim paid—or get less than you think you deserve—first complain to the company. The denial may be legitimate, and the insurer may explain policy provisions you didn't realize were included, but if you still believe there's an error, contact your state insurance department. Some state regulators are more effective than others in resolving consumer complaints, but it helps get the insurer's attention.

---

remember what you had when you're still in shock. Every year or so, take a video camera and go through each room, open closets and drawers then keep a copy of the videotape away from your home. Send a copy out of town—some Hurricane Katrina victims put copies of the inventory in a safe deposit box at their local bank, and then lost the paperwork when the storm destroyed their local bank, too.

Try to keep receipts for major purchases such as furniture, electronics, and appliances, which show how much you paid for the item. Keep in mind that the insurance payout will vary enormously depending on whether you bought replacement cost coverage or actual cash value coverage. Replacement cost coverage pays the amount it would cost to buy the item new today. Actual cash value subtracts depreciation from your original purchase price, leaving you with a lot less money to fill your home again.

Many insurance companies offer home inventory software, or you can download the Insurance Information Institute's Know Your Stuff inventory program from the Web site at *www.knowyourstuff.org*. Then keep a copy in a safe place away from your home and e-mail another copy to someone who lives far away, or keep a copy on a remote server on the Web. Update the inventory when you buy valuable new items.

If you don't have an inventory, you'll need to think of creative ways to document your losses. Some insurers will take your word for it to a certain extent, but others require you to provide evidence of everything before they'll pay for the damages. You may find the item in the background of family photos, or can dig up receipts, invoices, canceled checks, credit card slips, shipping receipts, or even instruction manuals and tax records (especially for any equipment you've deducted as a home office expense). The more evidence you can provide, the easier it will be to get your claim paid. Keep serial numbers of valuable items that are more likely to get stolen, like small electronics, and keep appraisals for high-end jewelry, artwork, and expensive collections.

You may be able to take a tax deduction for uninsured damage.

Damage not covered by insurance may be tax deductible, but you'll probably get less money than you expect. You can only deduct losses that aren't reimbursed by insurance, and the deduction is only available if you itemize your taxes. Then you generally need to subtract $100 and reduce the loss by 10 percent of your adjusted gross income, which means that if you earn $50,000 for the year, you won't be able to deduct the first $5,100 of your loss. This $100/10 percent requirement, however, was waived for Hurricane Katrina victims.

These types of losses are usually tax-deductible in the year they occur, so you'd need to wait until you file your taxes in order to report the loss, but if the damages occurred in a federal disaster area—like the counties in Louisiana, Mississippi, and Alabama affected by Hurricane Katrina—you get an additional option: You can either deduct the losses when you file that year's taxes by next April or amend your pervious year's return so you can get the money back faster. Katrina victims, for example, could either amend their 2004 return or file their losses with their 2005 return by April 2006. To file an amended return, download Form 1040x at the IRS's Web site (*www.irs.gov*), add the new information, and write the name of the disaster in red at the top. See the IRS Web site for a list of federal disaster areas. You can still deduct your losses if you aren't in a federal disaster area, but you'll have to do it when you file the taxes for that calendar year.

Even if you were in a federal disaster area, filing an amended return is not always the best option. You cannot write off the disaster loss if you took the standard deduction, for example, and you'll reach the 10 percent threshold faster in a year when your income is lower. For more information see IRS Publication 547, Casualties, Disasters, and Thefts (available at *www.irs.gov* or by calling 800-TAX-FORM).

TIPS FOR GETTING THE RIGHT HOMEOWNERS INSURANCE COVERAGE AT THE BEST PRICE

The rules for dealing with your homeowners insurance coverage have totally changed over the past few years. Most people now have too little homeowners insurance, the wrong types of coverage, and unknowingly do things that can get them dropped by their insurance company. Here's how to find—and keep—the right homeowners insurance:

- Don't file small claims. You may lose a valuable claims-free discount, which could boost your price by as much as 35 percent, even if the claim was for just a few hundred dollars. Even worse, many insurance companies now drop customers after filing just one or two small claims. After one insurer drops you, it can be tough to find affordable coverage anywhere. Raise your deductible to at least $1,000, which can lower your premiums by up to 30 percent and eliminate the temptation to file small claims that could cost you your coverage.

- Check your CLUE report, the database where insurance companies share information about you. Errors in your CLUE report can make it difficult to find affordable coverage anywhere and may hurt you if you're trying to sell your home. Also check a home's CLUE report before you buy, so you'll have a heads up about any problems that could cause insurers to shun the house.

- Compare prices from several companies, but don't switch insurers just to save a few dollars. You may lose a valuable claims-free discount, and a new insurer is more likely to drop you after filing a few small claims.

- Check out the insurer's complaint record with the state insurance department and national database. Homeowners insurance claims are some of the most complex to settle, and the experience can be very different from company to company—which you'll quickly discover in any Florida, Louisiana, or Mississippi neighborhood hit by hurricanes. It can be worthwhile to pay a few extra dollars in premiums if your insurer is less likely to hassle you at claim time.

- Most people have too little homeowners insurance because they haven't increased their insurance amount to keep up with home improvements or rising building costs. Have your agent or company reassess your home's replacement value every few years, hire an insurance appraiser, or use a Web tool that can help you estimate the value. It can cost just $50 to $100 to increase your coverage by $50,000.

- Homeowners insurance policies do not cover flooding, but you can get coverage through the National Flood Insurance Program (*www.floodsmart.gov*). The coverage can be valuable even if you don't live in a high-risk flood area—even before Hurricane Katrina, 25 percent of all flood-loss claims were filed in low-to-moderate risk areas. You can generally get $100,000 of coverage for $230 to $860, unless you're in a particularly high-risk area. Also consider adding earthquake coverage, sewage backup coverage, and building and ordinance coverage (for people with older homes), which aren't automatically covered in most homeowners insurance policies. Buy extra coverage for jewelry and other valuables worth more than $1,000.

- It's important—and inexpensive—to buy extra coverage if you have a home office or rent an apartment. Also consider an umbrella policy to protect your family from expensive lawsuits; you can generally add $1 million in liability coverage for just $250 to $350 per year.

CHAPTER 4

AUTO INSURANCE

■ ■ ■

One of the easiest ways to free up more than $1,000 from your budget is to attack your auto insurance. Prices vary so much from company to company, that it's easy to save a few hundred dollars just by shopping around. Now is a particularly good time to search for a better deal—several large insurers just changed the way they set their rates, which can result in big cost savings for people with good driving and credit records. Some people with bad driving records may finally find better deals, too, now that big-name insurers are less likely to reject them. It's much easier for everyone to compare rates from several companies than it was just a few years ago.

You can shave money off your premiums by taking advantage of every discount you deserve, including little-known price breaks that many people overlook. Dropping redundant coverage can cut your premiums some more, and knowing a few key strategies for dealing with high-risk situations—like when your teenager starts driving—can help you minimize the price hikes.

Piece all of these steps together and you can cut your premiums in half without sacrificing any coverage.

You can save hundreds of dollars just by shopping around. The price range can be huge—for the exact same coverage.

Comparing rates from several companies is the most important strategy when searching for a good deal on auto insurance. The price range can be huge from one company to the next for the exact same person and car. Too many people end up overpaying for auto insurance—and getting absolutely nothing extra in return—just because they're too lazy to see what else is out there.

The annual premiums can vary by almost $1,500, for example, for a married 45-year-old couple who lives in Chicago, drives a 2004 Toyota Highlander and a 2002 Volkswagen Passat, and has $500 comprehensive and collision deductibles. They could pay as much as $3,476 per year or as little as $1,986 for the same coverage, just by picking a different company. The price range can be even wider for families with young drivers. Add a 16-year-old son to that Chicago couple's policy and the price range goes up to $2,417 on the low end or $5,066 on the high end—and that's if the son only drives the Passat occasionally and everyone has a spotless driving record. Interestingly, the company with the lowest rate for the couple had one of the highest rates when the son was added.

That family could cut its auto insurance costs in half without losing any coverage. In fact, they don't need to make much effort at all; all they need to do is switch companies. It's about one of the easiest ways to free up more than $2,500 without having to do much work.

It's a good idea to shop around and compare rates from a few companies every few years or whenever your auto insurance needs change—if, for example, you buy a new car, move to a different area, or if your child gets her license or moves away from home. Those are all key events that can affect your auto insurance rate, and each company looks at them differently. Some are more lenient to families with kids. Others may add a big surcharge if you buy a sports car or move to the city. As the Chicago family discovered, the company that offers the lowest rate in one situation may charge some of the highest prices in another.

The price differences are based, in part, on the insurer's profitability, business model, and method of assessing various risks. They can vary widely, though, because they depend a lot on the insurance company's experience with its customers. If people who live in your area or have your type of car tend to have more accidents at one company, then they'll charge you a higher rate than a company that hasn't received many claims from people with a similar profile.

Insurance rates are highly personalized based on hundreds of factors—a lot more than insurers looked at just a few years ago. Most insurers consider the type of car, your driving record, where you live, where the car is parked, how far you drive, whether or not you use the car to commute, your age, your marital status, and even consider your occupation and credit record. That's why your neighbor may be paying a very different price than you, and the list of companies offering their family the lowest rate may not look anything like yours.

The only way to see who's offering you the best deal is to get price quotes from several companies. There's good news: It's now a lot easier to compare auto insurance rates from several insurers than it was just a few years ago.

A few states' insurance departments, like California, Texas, New Jersey, and New York, publish rate comparisons online. These price lists are for hypothetical people and won't have a lot to do with the specific price you'd get yourself, but they can give you a good head start and help you identify companies that tend to have competitive rates for people like you, which are worthwhile to contact.

You can get price quotes online from many insurance companies, such as Progressive, Allstate, and State Farm, or go to an insurance marketplace like InsWeb or Insure.com, which can help you find rates from several insurers. You can get online quotes quickly, but you won't get the exact price unless you give them permission to check your credit record and driving report. It's a good way to see how several companies' prices compare when you're starting your search, then narrow down the list before giving the insurer your personal information.

Insurers with online capabilities can check your records immediately after getting your Social Security number and the car's vehicle identification number and give you a specific price. Progressive, for example, even provides a spreadsheet showing the cost breakdowns for various coverage levels, so you can easily see how much you can save by raising your deductible from $500 to $1,000 or how little it costs to raise your liability coverage form $100,000 to $250,000.

You can get personalized attention—plus a lot of help with insurance-buying strategies—by working with an independent insurance agent. These agents generally deal with many companies and know from experience the ones that tend to have the best deals for people in your area, with your type of car and other criteria. Long-time independent agents are also very familiar with the insurers' customer service reputations, and tend to steer clients away from companies that hassle customers on claims. It's particularly helpful to work with an independent agent if you've had any tickets or accidents in the past five years or are adding a teenage driver to your policy, and can see an even wider price range from company to company. You can find an independent agent through the Independent Insurance Agents and Brokers of America (*www.iiaba.org*).

A few companies, like State Farm, don't sell through independent agents, so you'll need to get quotes directly from their Web site or work with a local agent. If a family member is in the military, you might get a good rate from USAA, which only sells directly instead of through agents (*www.usaa.com* or 800-365-USAA). USAA surveyed new policyholders in mid-2004, for example, and found that the average customer saved $400 per year just by switching companies.

It isn't as dangerous to change auto insurance companies, or submit claims, as it is with homeowners insurance, but you might lose a good driver or long-time customer discount for switching companies, and your long-time insurer may cut you more slack if you have an accident. Insuring your home and car with the same company can give you a discount of up to 15 percent on both policies. So if you switch to another car insurer, don't forget that your homeowners insurance rate may go up, too.

Don't just shop based on price. Check out the insurer's complaint record at your state insurance department Web site and the National Association of Insurance Commissioners' Consumer Information Source (*www.naic.org/cis*). For more information on researching a company's customer complaint records, see the homeowners insurance chapter.

Now is a particularly good time to shop around. Some insurers are changing their rules—which can lower your rates by up to 25 percent.

Several major auto insurance companies, including State Farm, Allstate, and Progressive, are in the midst of changing the way they set their rates, which could lead to big savings for you.

Until recently, most auto insurance companies based their premiums on just a handful of variables, such as your type of car, where you live, your age, and your driving record. Many still focus on those criteria, but because of advanced computing capabilities, insurers can now consider many more factors when assessing the risk that you'll have a claim, based on the number of claims they've paid out for people with similar features. For example, instead of just looking at damage and theft claim payments for the car you're considering, which has been a key factor in determining collision and comprehensive premiums for many years, they're also looking at the cost of injury claims to passengers in that type of car, and more recently started looking at claim payment amounts for damages that car does to other vehicles and their occupants, which now is a key factor when pricing your liability coverage.

They're looking more closely at the number of miles you drive, not just whether it's more or less than 7,500, and, when allowed under state law, some are looking at your credit report in excruciating detail. In the past, they'd generally review your credit report primarily to see whether it was good or bad, but now they're looking at dozens of data points within your report—such as how many payments you've made 30 days late, 60 days late, or 90 days late, for example, and how that compares to claims records for people with similar late payments.

Because of their powerful computer systems, insurers are able to assess all of these pieces of information about yourself, your cars, driving record, credit score, and where you live and compare it to their claims records to assess your risk almost immediately. Allstate went from seven to 384 pricing tiers. State Farm is in the midst of shifting from five tiers to more than 100. Progressive is making similar changes.

These insurers are now able to do a much better job of matching people up with their expected risks, rather than lumping them into just a handful of categories. As a result, people with some of the lowest risk factors may see their rate fall by about 25 percent, says Allstate spokesperson Michael Trevino.

However, the flip side is true, too. People with moderately riskier profiles might see their rates increase as a result of these new pricing rules, when the insurer discovers they were on the riskier end of the pricing tier. These people may benefit from selecting an insurer that hasn't changed its rules yet. The only way to find out which is better for you is to compare price quotes from several companies, including some that have changed their rules and some that haven't.

The rates can vary a lot even among companies that have changed their pricing rules, because each one is looking carefully at different variables and comparing it to a different pool of claims data. It's a good idea for everyone to shop around now—either online or through an independent agent.

These rule changes can also be surprisingly good news for higher-risk drivers, who might finally find it easier to get coverage with a mainstream auto insurance company, rather than getting stuck with an impaired-risk insurer (one specializing in high-risk drivers) that might charge extremely high rates for mediocre coverage. Now that some insurers are doing a better job of assessing their risks, they feel comfortable that they have enough information about some of these risky drivers and can price their policies accordingly. The price may be high, but at least they won't be turned down—and the cost and coverage may still be a lot better than with the high-risk insurance companies.

Your credit score can make a huge difference in your auto insurance price—even more than it had in the past.

You can have a great driving record and safe car but still end up with a high auto insurance rate. Why? It could be because of your credit score.

Your credit score is a number that most lenders use to help predict the likelihood that you'll repay your mortgage, car loans, credit card balances, and other debts. The score is based on information from your credit report, such as whether you've made any late loan payments, how much money you owe, the length of your credit history, and how much new credit you've taken on recently, and then run through a complex set of calculations to translate all of that information into a score that lenders can use to assess your credit risk.

Most auto insurance companies started using credit scores a few years ago as one of many factors to consider when setting your insurance rate. As insurers add more pricing tiers and expand the criteria they consider, the details of your credit record can have an even greater impact on your rate.

This might seem strange. What does your credit record have to do with auto insurance? It actually has a lot to do with it. When studying their claims records over the past several years, insurers discovered a correlation between credit scores and auto insurance claims; people with poor credit scores are more likely than people with good scores to file auto insurance claims. In 2004, upon request from the state legislature after a spate of bad publicity, the Texas Department of Insurance conducted its own study to see if this was really true, and verified the claim. After studying the claims records of 2 million insurance policies, the insurance department found "the difference in claims experience by credit score was substantial," according to the regulator's report. The claim experience for the 10 percent of policyholders with the worst credit scores was 1.5 to 2 times greater than that of the 10 percent of policyholders with the best credit scores, for both auto and homeowners insurance (credit scores are generally taken into account when pricing both types of policies). Moreover, drivers with the best credit scores are involved in about 40 percent fewer accidents than those with the worst credit scores.

A few states limit insurers' use of credit scores when setting their premiums or deciding who to insure, based on concern that the practice could discriminate against low-income people and minorities, and a few insurers don't use credit scores in their pricing. Most of them do, though, and improving your score can save you money on your auto and homeowners insurance.

First, make sure there aren't any errors on your credit report. You can now order one free credit report every 12 months from each of the three major credit bureaus—Equifax, Experian, and TransUnion. Go to *www.annualcreditreport.com* or call 877-322-8228 to order. Each credit bureau's Web site (*www.equifax.com, www.experian.com,* and *www.transunion.com*) lists details about how to correct any errors (see Figure 4.1).

Then check your insurance score. This is the credit score insurers use when determining your rates, which is a bit different than the credit score that lenders use when you apply for a loan. You can get a copy from ChoiceTrust (*www.choicetrust.com*) for $12.95. The report shows you your score, how it compares to other consumers in the United States, and whether it's considered a good or bad score.

While you're at the ChoiceTrust Web site, check your CLUE report, the comprehensive loss underwriting exchange report, where insurers share information with each other about claims paid on your homeowners and auto insurance policies over the past five years. See

FIGURE 4.1 How to Check Your Credit Report

You can now get a free copy of your credit record every 12 months from each of the three major credit bureaus. To order your free reports, go to *www.annualcreditreport .com* or call 877-322-8228.

You can also order your reports directly from the credit bureaus, contact them to fix any errors, or visit their Web sites for more information and strategies for improving your record:

- Equifax—*www.equifax.com;* 800-685-1111
- Experian—*www.experian.com;* 888-397-3742
- TransUnion—*www.transunion.com;* 800-916-8800

To order a copy of your insurance score, the version of your credit score that many insurers use, go to *www.ChoiceTrust.com.*

To get a copy of your credit score that most lenders use or learn about improving your score, see *www.MyFico.com.*

Chapter 3 for more information about how your CLUE report can affect your insurance rates.

Your insurance score is different from the credit score that lenders use, but you can get a lot of good advice about improving your credit record at the Fair Isaac Web site, the company that creates the credit scores many lenders use. See *www.myfico.com* for more information.

Raising your deductible can cut your premiums significantly.

After you've shopped around for the best rate, raising your deductible can cut your costs even further. It's an easy way to lower your rate without taking on much extra risk yourself. Raising your deductible from $250 to $1,000, for example, can cut your premium by 15 percent or more and make you less likely to file small claims that could show up on your CLUE report and eventually lead to a rate increase. Then you can use the cost savings to boost your liability coverage, which can make tens of thousands of dollars worth of difference in your protection amount.

That 45-year-old Chicago couple could lower their rate by $284 per year just by raising their deductibles from $250 to $1,000. Because the price is so much higher for families with young drivers, raising your deductibles can cut your rates even more if you're insuring teenage drivers. Boosting their deductibles to $1,000 would cut their rate by nearly $690 with their 16-year-old son on their policy. If you don't have any accidents that year, you'd pocket the entire savings yourself, and even if you do have an accident, the premium savings would still offset the extra cost. Be sure to keep enough money in your emergency fund to cover the potential out-of-pocket costs.

If you have an old car worth less than a few thousand dollars, consider dropping collision and comprehensive coverage (also called "physical damage coverage") entirely. You may be paying more in premiums than you could possibly get back from the insurance company in claims. The maximum your insurer will pay to replace your car is the depreciated value of your car minus the deductible. If your car is worth less than a few thousand dollars, your physical damage premiums may be almost as much as the amount you'd get from your insurer if you totaled your car. Each insurer has its own calculations for valuing cars, but for an idea of how much yours may be worth, check out the used-car values for cars like yours at Kelley Blue Book (*www.kbb.com*).

Dropping physical damage coverage, however, may not be an option if you have a car loan, and your lender may also limit the size of your deductible.

Many people don't have enough liability coverage. It's incredibly inexpensive to boost your liability coverage by tens of thousands of dollars.

After you raise your deductible, then you can use your premium savings to make sure you have enough liability coverage. Liability coverage includes several potential costs. The bodily injury portion covers medical bills and lost wages for anyone you hurt in a car accident, as well as any legal bills for pain and suffering and lawyer's fees. The property damage portion covers damage to anything other than your own car—usually the amount you'll need to fix the other person's car or anything else you hit.

Ignore your state minimum liability requirements; they're usually dangerously low; in many, it's about $25,000 per person/ $50,000 per accident and $15,000 for property damage. Because of the high price of lawsuits, medical expenses, and the increasing cost of replacing a crashed car, it's a good idea to carry at least $100,000 in liability coverage per person/$300,000 per accident and $100,000 for property damage (often listed on the policy as 100/300/100).

That Chicago couple would pay $1,132 per year for 100/300/100 in liability coverage on their two cars ($792 on the Highlander and $340 on the Passat). Boosting that coverage to $250,000 per person/ $500,000 per accident/$250,000 for property damage would only cost them a mere $40 extra per year—for more than $150,000 in extra coverage.

Consider raising your liability coverage even higher if you have a teenage driver, which is one of the biggest causes of liability claims. Once you hit the maximum limits on your auto and homeowners insurance policy, you can get an umbrella policy to boost your coverage even further. It generally costs about $250 to $350 per year to increase your coverage by $1 million, which covers you for both homeowners and auto liability.

Medical-payments coverage may be redundant—but don't drop it entirely.

Medical-payments coverage generally pays from $1,000 to $10,000 in medical and funeral expenses for each injured person in your car, regardless of who is at fault. It sounds important, but it actually duplicates other coverage that most people already have. Your health insurance will generally pay those bills if someone in your family is hurt, and your passengers' health insurer may pay for their injuries. In addition, the premiums for this coverage have increased significantly over the past few years along with rising medical costs.

However, it's a good idea to keep some medical-payments coverage—$1,000 to $5,000—to cover your health insurance deductible and out-of-pocket expenses, especially if you have a high-deductible health insurance policy. The medical-payments coverage can also help if you tend to drive around other people who may not have health insurance. If anything happens to them, the at-fault driver's liability coverage could eventually pay their bills, but it can take a while to establish blame. Your medical-payments coverage can help cover your passengers' medical expenses, no matter who ends up being at fault.

The Chicago couple would pay $104 per year for $5,000 of medical payments coverage, but only $36 per year for $2,000 of the coverage, a premium savings of $68 by cutting some redundant coverage.

Get all the discounts you deserve. You may be able to cut your rate in half without giving up any coverage—but only if you know to ask.

Auto insurers offer a ton of discounts that can cut your premiums significantly, but the insurance company won't automatically give them to you; you need to know to ask. The type and size of discounts varies a lot by company and state, and may only affect part of your policy. Ask your insurance company or agent about its discounts. Most insurers' Web sites list available discounts, too—State Farm's Web site even lets you search for the discounts specifically offered in your state (see Figure 4.2 for a list of common discounts).

Taking advantage of several discounts can be great, but don't forget the bottom line: How much you'll actually pay in premiums. Some companies may offer higher premiums but more discounts;

FIGURE 4.2 Common Auto Insurance Discounts

Taking advantage of every discount you deserve can lower your auto insurance rate by hundreds of dollars, without having to make any sacrifices. Discounts vary a lot from company to company and state to state, but here are some common ones:

- *Multiple policies*—Having both auto and homeowners insurance with the same company can lower your premiums by 15 percent on both policies, making the discount twice as valuable as it looks at first.
- *Good driver*—You may get up to a 20 percent discount if everyone on the policy hasn't had an at-fault accident or moving violation in the past three or five years.
- *Low mileage*—You may get a 5 percent to 10 percent discount if you drive fewer than 7,500 miles per year.
- *Good student*—You may be able to save as much as 30 percent if your child has a B average or better or is in the top 20 percent of his or her class.
- *Driving course*—Drivers age 55 and older may get a discount for completing a defensive driving or mature driver improvement course (the rules vary by state). Young drivers may receive discounts for participating in certain courses and programs, too.
- *Retiree discount*—You may get a price break if you're 55 or older and not employed.
- *Multicar discount*—Having more than one car on the policy can cut your premiums by more than 10 percent.
- *Safety devices*—You may get a discount if your car has antilock brakes, air bags, automatic seat belts, and daytime running lights.
- *Antitheft devices*—The type of alarm system you have can make a big difference in the size of the discount. Check with your insurance company before installing a new alarm system to make sure it qualifies for the discount.
- *Other discounts*—You may also get a discount for carpooling, for staying with the same company for five years or more, or for buying coverage through your employer, professional, or alumni association.

---

others may offer lower premiums to everyone but not as many discounts. When comparing companies, it's most important to compare total costs.

The type of car can make a big difference—even more than in the past. And it's easy to check out its insurance costs ahead of time.

The type of car you own always made a big difference in the price you'd pay for collision and comprehensive coverage—insurers charge higher physical damage rates for cars that cost a lot to repair and are frequently stolen—but now they're also looking more carefully at the damages your car can do to other cars and their passengers, which affects the cost for liability coverage and medical payments or personal injury protection. The difference is obvious in SUVs, which tend to hold up well in collisions but often cause more damage to other cars. As a result, an SUV may have relatively low premiums for collision coverage, but higher costs for bodily injury and property damage coverage.

Several insurance companies have tools that help you look up the relative cost of insurance for the cars you're considering. Allstate's Make and Model Comparison Tool (in the Tools section of the Allstate Web site) shows whether the car's insurance costs for liability and physical damage coverage are better, worse, or average compared to other makes and models. A Ford Expedition, for example, has a much better than average physical damage rating and a better than average liability rating. A Ford Mustang, on the other hand, has a worse than average liability rating and a much worse than average physical damage rating.

State Farm's Web site (*www.statefarm.com,* type "vehicle ratings" in the search engine) goes into more detail, grading cars on their relative insurance costs in three categories. State Farm has been using claims data for damage and theft for many years to help set the prices for a car's collision and comprehensive coverage, and charging higher rates for the types of cars that have cost them most in claims. You can look up State Farm's damage and theft index grade for the type of car you're considering. If the company's payments for that model's damage and theft claims are lower than average, then the premiums are generally 10 to 40 percent lower than the standard collision and comprehensive premiums for cars in that price range. If the claims in those areas are higher than average, then the premiums tend to be 10 to 40 percent higher than similar cars. Four years ago, State Farm also started looking at the cost of claims involving injury to the occupants of the insured car. Depending on the results, some makes and models qualify for vehicle safety discounts, typically ranging from 0 percent to 40 percent off the premiums for medical payments or personal injury protection coverage. Just recently, State Farm also started looking at claims payments it has made on that type of car for damages to other cars and their occupants. The result, its liability rating index affects the car's liability premiums.

You'll also get detailed car-safety information for the car you're considering, including grades for the car's front, rear and side crash test results, from the Insurance Institute for Highway Safety (*www.carsafety.org*). The 2006 Top Safety Pick awards include the Ford Five Hundred and Mercury Montego for large cars, the Subaru Legacy and Saab 9-3 for midsize cars, and the Honda Civic for small cars (see Figure 4.3).

You can find a list of the most stolen vehicles in the United States from the National Insurance Crime Bureau (*www.nicb.org*). Older cars without good security devices tend to be riskiest. The 1995 Honda Civic topped the list in 2004, followed by the 1989 Toyota Camry, the 1991 Honda Accord, and the 1994 Dodge Caravan.

FIGURE 4.3 2006 Safest Cars

The Insurance Institute for Highway Safety picked the following cars as the safest models for 2006, based on protection for people in front, side, and rear crashes:

Large Cars
- Gold Award: Ford Five Hundred and Mercury Montego (with optional side airbags)
- Silver Award: Audi A6

Midsize Cars
- Gold Award: Saab 9-3 and Subaru Legacy
- Silver Award: Audi A3, Audi A4, Chevrolet Malibu (with optional side airbags), Volkswagen Jetta, and Volkswagen Passat

Small Cars
- Gold Award: Honda Civic

Source: Insurance Institute for Highway Safety

Each insurer's specific costs will vary based on their own claims experience, but these tools can give you a general idea of how your car's insurance costs stack up. Choosing a safe car with low insurance costs is particularly valuable when you have a teenage driver, and will need all the help you can get to find lower rates.

A few key moves can lower your teenager's rate by hundreds—or even thousands—of dollars.

It's always scary to be the parent of a new driver—and it's even scarier when you get the first auto insurance bill with your child on the policy. Adding a teenage daughter to your auto insurance policy can boost your price by 50 percent; adding a teenage son can double your premiums even before they get their first ticket or accident, according to the Insurance Information Institute.

Because teenage drivers are young and inexperienced (and often easily distracted) they tend to have a lot more accidents than everyone else does. In 2001, 39 percent of all deaths of 16- to 19-year-olds were related to motor vehicles. The insurance claims for collision and injury on cars driven by teenagers are more than double those driven only by adults, according to the Insurance Institute for Highway Safety. So it's no surprise that adding a teenager to your policy can wreak havoc with your rates. That's what happened to the Chicago couple. Adding a 16-year-old son to their policy hiked their rate from $1,986 to more than $5,000 per year.

They don't actually need to pay nearly that much for coverage. A few key moves can lower your rate significantly. When your kids are teenagers, you need to aggressively seek out discounts and make the most of strategies to lower your cost. Cobbling together several discounts and cost-saving strategies can cut your child's premiums in half.

First, shop around. Insurance companies have very different views towards teenage drivers. Some don't really want to take on the risk, so they send your premiums sky high when your child joins you on your policy. Others try to keep their policies relatively affordable for young families, with hopes that they'll attract business away from other companies. Some offer discounts for young drivers, like a good-student discount, while others don't. In addition, they tend to divide teenagers into different groups. Some companies have different rate classes for every year—charging one incredibly high rate for 16-year-olds, a little less for 17-year-olds, and even less for 18- and 19-year-olds with good driving records. Others group teenagers together, making 16- to 18-year-olds one rate class, and 19- to 20-year-olds another. Those companies may offer better deals for the youngest drivers because they temper the prices a bit for drivers with an extra year or two of experience.

Interestingly, the company that offered one of the lowest rates to the Chicago couple before their son got his license ended up offering one of the highest rates—more than $5,000—after they added him to their policy, but a few other companies would charge the family less than $3,000. Switching to another company could free an extra $2,000. You need to shop around and compare prices every year or so after your child starts driving, but the savings do need to be significant in order to merit the switch. A long-time insurer may be more understanding if your child has an accident, and may be worth sticking with if you'd only be saving a few hundred dollars.

The car your child drives will make a big difference in the price of insurance. It is particularly important that young drivers have safe cars, both for the parents' peace of mind and to help lower the insurance premiums, because they are more likely to be involved in an accident. Your best bet is usually a midsized car that isn't too valuable, but isn't too old, either. Cars more than six- to ten-years-old may be missing today's safety features, such as airbags, that can help reduce the cost of accidents. Check out insurance costs for various models on the Allstate and State Farm Web sites and review crash test ratings at the Insurance Institute for Highway Safety Web site (*www.carsafety.org*).

Your rates will be lowest if you add your child to your safest car as only an occasional driver, with the parent still driving that car most of the time. Even if he has his own car, it's generally less-expensive to keep your child on your own policy rather than have him buy his own insurance, so he can benefit from your discounts for insuring multiple drivers and cars. Many insurers don't want to have anything to do with teenagers on their own, and may reject kids who apply for their own policies, but it doesn't hurt to run the numbers each way and see which works out better in your situation. This may also be a good time to start working with an independent insurance agent, who knows how many companies view teenage drivers and can run the numbers for several variations on the coverage.

Because your rates are so high anyway, you'll save a lot of money by raising your deductibles to at least $1,000. The Chicago family could cut its rates by nearly $688 per year by raising their deductibles from $250 to $1,000. When the value of the car drops below a few thousand dollars, consider dropping collision and com-prehensive coverage entirely because you're probably paying more in premiums than the maximum payout you could get. That easily could cut another few hundred dollars off your premium. Mean-while, use that extra money to increase your liability coverage, which you'll definitely need with a young driver around. For less than $200 per year, the Chicago family could boost its liability cov-erage from 100/300/100 to 250/500/250. With a young driver on board, it's also a good idea to consider an umbrella liability policy, which can offer $1 million or more of extra liability coverage after you max out your auto and homeowners insurance limits. You can generally get a $1 million umbrella policy for $250 to $350, although the cost may be a bit higher when you have a youthful driver because the odds become much greater that it will have to pay out. The largest portion of an insurer's umbrella liability claims are generally from car accidents involving teenagers.

Aggressively seek out discounts, and make great efforts to qualify for them. Most companies offer young drivers a good student discount, cutting their rates by up to 30 percent if they maintain a B average.

Some offer a discount for driver's education classes (although fewer do now than they did in the past because the standard driver's education programs didn't improve teenagers' driving records as much as expected). Also make the most of your family's other discounts, such as by insuring all of your cars with the same company, keeping your auto and homeowners insurance with the same company, and having everyone in the family maintain a spotless driving record (see Figure 4.4).

Find out if your insurer offers special programs to young drivers in return for an extra discount. Taking the time to participate can save your kid big money. State Farm offers a Steer Clear Driver Discount in some states, which gives a discount to all male and unmarried female drivers under age 25 who have had no at-fault accidents or moving violations in the past three years and have completed a special program administered by a State Farm agent that includes a video presentation, reading a safe-driving magazine, and completing a driver's log to document driving experiences.

FIGURE 4.4 Valuable Discounts

Families with teenagers can cut their rates significantly by taking advantage of several discounts and cost-saving strategies. The specific results will vary a lot by company and person, but here's how one 17-year-old boy can cut his rate from $4,056 down to $2,210 per year. These calculations assume he lives in Montgomery County, Maryland, and is the primary driver of a 2001 Subaru Legacy with $250,000 in liability coverage and a $200 deductible for comprehensive and $500 for collision coverage.

- Good-student discount reduces his rate by $700 per year
- Three-year accident-free discount for his family reduces his rate by $332 per year
- Participating in the insurance company's young driver education program reduces his rate by $354 per year
- Keeping his family's auto and homeowners policies with the same insurance company reduces his rate by $460 per year
- **Total savings:** $1,846 per year

He could also lower his rate by boosting his deductibles to $1,000 each, and can cut the price by more than $450 if he's only an occasional driver of that car.

Source: The Insurance Information Institute

You'll finally get a big discount if your student moves more than 100 miles away from home for college and doesn't take his car, but because he's still on your policy, he'll be covered when he returns home for vacation or if he borrows or rents a car. If he does take a car with him to school, the premium could increase or decrease depending on the location of the school and where the car is parked. Still, it is generally a better deal to keep him on your policy rather than getting his own.

The most important strategy is to maintain a spotless driving record. If you think the quotes you get when your kid starts driving are bad, then you really don't want to see what can happen after your kid has an accident or a speeding ticket, which can raise your rates even higher—and will keep them that way for at least three years.

Fighting a ticket can save you a lot more money than you realize.

Getting a traffic ticket is expensive. Not only will you have to pay a big fine but also your insurer could raise your rates for three to five years as a result. One moving violation can cost you any good-driver discount you've been getting—worth up to 20 percent—although some companies let your first ticket slide. The insurer can also add a surcharge onto your policy—$150 per ticket added to your policy for three years in some states, for example, or a 20 percent price hike in others. A few states give you a free ride on one ticket within three years, but then allow insurers to boost your rate after that. A bad-enough driving record can land you in the higher-risk arm of the insurance company, which charges higher premiums, or could get you dropped.

The best strategy, of course, is to avoid getting tickets, but even if you do end up with a moving violation, you might be able to make it disappear in the insurance company's eyes. It can pay to go to court and fight the ticket. You could win for good reason or your case may be dismissed if the police officer doesn't show up. You may still benefit even if you have to plead guilty. If you have a good driving record, some judges may reduce the fine and the points, or give you probation. If you don't get in trouble within the next year, the ticket may never show up on your record, and in some states, you can keep the ticket off your record by going to traffic school, although you may only be able to use that strategy once every year or two.

The effort can be worth it. Even if you get stuck paying the full fine, if the judge reduces the number of points you could end up preserving a safe-driver discount, avoid an insurance surcharge, and save a few hundred dollars in premiums for three years or more.

You may not have enough insurance to pay off your loan. But you can buy inexpensive extra coverage to make up the difference.

You could owe your lender thousands of dollars if you total your car—even if you have auto insurance. Insurers generally pay up to the car's depreciated value, which could be thousands of dollars less than you owe your lender if you crash it in the first year or two, especially if you put down less than 20 percent when you bought your car, have a loan that lasts for four years or more, and have a car that depreciates rapidly. The situation, called an "upside down loan" because you owe the lender more than the car is worth, is becoming quite common—especially as more people stretch out the loan for five and six years and make down payments as low as $0. The situation gets worse when competitive new-car rebates and financing deals make many used cars less attractive, causing them to lose value much faster than they had in the past. Some five-year loans are upside down for as long as three years, meaning you'll owe the lender money from your own pocket if you total the car, even if you have full insurance.

Several lenders, car dealers, and auto insurance companies offer gap insurance (also called "loan/lease payoff") to pay the difference between the car's actual cash value (the depreciated value the insurer generally pays out if the car is totaled) and the amount you owe the lender. This coverage has been available to car leasers for quite a while; now it's being sold to more new-car buyers, too. The coverage can be valuable for at least a year or two if you could end up owing a few thousand dollars more than the insurer will pay. GMAC Insurance's average gap insurance claim, for example, is about $3,000.

Some insurers, such as Progressive, let you add a rider to your auto policy that will pay up to 25 percent more than a car's depreciated value if it's totaled. The extra coverage costs about $50 per car each year. Other companies charge a flat fee of $14 to $20 per year for the coverage, no matter how big the gap is. A few companies provide extra coverage in their standard policies with no additional charge. MetLife, for example, will pay the full cost to buy a new car if you total your car within the first year and have driven less than 15,000 miles.

Many lenders and dealers offer policies that can fill in the gap, too. Dealers generally charge up to $500 or $600 for the coverage (the specifics vary by state) as a one-time charge you can add to your loan balance. The coverage lasts for the life of the loan, but you may want to drop it early if you can get a partial refund after the gap shrinks.

If you made a down payment of 20 percent or more and your loan is for 36 months or less, you probably don't have a gap problem. People with lower down payments and longer loan terms should go to Kelley Blue Book's Web site (*www.kbb.com*) and see how much one-year-old versions of the car you're considering are selling for used. Look at the "private party" numbers and pick "good" rather than "excellent" condition. Insurers generally pay less than the blue book amount if you total your car, with the specific value based on the prices for similar used cars sold in your area. You can generally get a good idea of the insurer's payout amount if you subtract about 20 percent from the Kelley Blue Book used-car values. Then, look at the lender's amortization table, showing how much of your loan's principal is paid off each month, or run your numbers through the "How Much Will My Vehicle Payments Be?" calculator at *www.Kiplinger.com* to see how much you'd still owe after one year. If you'd still owe a few thousand dollars more than your insurer will pay, then gap coverage can be worthwhile for the first year or two of the loan. Do the math again after two years. As time passes, the size of the gap shrinks, and the premiums may no longer be worth it after you've paid off a bigger chunk of the loan.

Don't drop your coverage entirely if you won't be driving for a while.

Do you think you're going to save money by dropping your auto insurance if you aren't going to be driving for a while? That strategy can backfire because many insurance companies require you to have continuous coverage. Even if you haven't been driving for a few months, if you've been out of the country, for example, you may have a tough time finding insurance, or paying a decent rate, when you return.

That's what happened to quite a few soldiers who returned from serving in Iraq. Many of the unmarried soldiers decided to store their cars and drop their coverage when they were deployed, but when they returned, some ended up with penalties because they didn't have continuous insurance coverage or they lost their long-term customer and good-customer discounts. Others had a difficult time finding coverage at all.

In many states, insurance companies can penalize people who don't have continuous coverage. The reason is because they worry that the car owners had been driving without insurance. After a lot of bad publicity, many insurers stopped penalizing the war veterans for dropping their coverage while deployed, but everyone else needs to be careful before dropping their coverage. There are other ways to save money if you aren't going to be driving for a while, while avoiding potential problems in the future.

Even if your car will be in storage while you're gone, it's a good idea to keep some coverage—to make it easier to resume coverage when you return, and to protect your car if it's stolen, vandalized, destroyed in a fire, or damaged in any other way while you're away. One way is to get "lay up coverage," which eliminates all coverage except comprehensive and insures your car against theft, fire, and other damage even while it isn't being driven. This can lower your premiums by as much as 75 percent.

However, many states won't allow you to eliminate liability coverage entirely unless you turn in your license plates, and many lenders will require you to keep a minimum level of coverage until your loan is paid off. In that case, you can still lower your premiums significantly by reducing your liability coverage to the state's minimum limits (generally around $25,000 per person/$50,000 per accident and $15,000 for property damage) and boosting your deductibles as high as they can go. This way you'll also have some coverage if you rent or borrow a car. At the very least, tell your insurer that you won't be driving for a while and you may qualify for a low-mileage discount.

If you sell your car while you're gone, consider switching to a nonowner policy, which some insurers offer for people who drive occasionally but don't own their own car. This can cut your rates significantly, keep you covered if you borrow or rent a car, and give you continuous coverage that can make it easier to get a policy next time you buy a car.

If you dropped your coverage and your insurer tries to raise your rate when you restart your policy, explain why you weren't driving— sometimes that can make a difference. Otherwise, shop around and see if you can get a better deal elsewhere. There are wide variations in the way companies treat a break in coverage.

TIPS FOR GETTING THE RIGHT AUTO INSURANCE AT THE BEST PRICE

It's easy to lower your auto insurance premiums by hundreds of dollars if you shop around, get all the discounts you deserve, and know a few key strategies that can cut your costs even further. Several large insurers are in the midst of changing the way they set rates, which makes it a particularly good time to check out your auto insurance options:

- Compare rates from several auto insurance companies. The price range can be huge for the exact same person, and the insurer that offers your neighbor the best rate may actually be the most expensive one for you. Shop around online, through an agent, directly through a few companies, and see if your state insurance department has price comparisons, too. Only switch insurers, though, if you can cut your costs significantly. Otherwise, you may lose a valuable claims-free or long-term customer discount and be more likely to get punished if you have a ticket or an accident.

- Improve your credit score, which now makes a big difference in your auto insurance rate. Order your free credit reports at *www.AnnualCreditReport.com* and fix any errors. Check out your insurance score at *www.ChoiceTrust.com* and your credit score at *www.MyFico.com,* which also includes helpful tips for improving the number.

- Raise your deductible to at least $1,000 for comprehensive and collision coverage, or drop that coverage entirely if your car is only worth a few thousand dollars. Boost your liability coverage to at least $100,000 per person/$250,000 per accident/$100,000 for property damage, limit medical payments coverage to $1,000 to $5,000, and make sure you get credit for all of the discounts you deserve. Check out your car's safety rating before you buy.

- A few key moves can cut your teenager's rate in half. Keep your child on your own policy, pair him with a safe car, and only make him an occasional driver, raise deductibles as high as you can (or drop comprehensive and collision coverage entirely if it's an inexpensive car), sign up for driver's education or any special programs the insurer offers to improve kids' driving and lower rates, make sure he maintains good grades, have everyone in the household be particularly careful to avoid accidents and tickets when you have a teenage driver (which can boost the rates for everyone), and let the insurance company know if he moves more than 100 miles away for college and doesn't take his car.

■ If you apply a low down payment when you buy your car, extend your loan over five years or more, and have a car that depreciates quickly, then your insurance may not be enough to pay off your loan if you total your car. In that case, consider buying inexpensive "gap coverage" that can make up the difference for a few years.

■ Don't drop your coverage entirely if you won't be driving for a while. Insurers typically boost rates or make it tough to get new coverage if you've gone for a while without insurance. Either drop everything but comprehensive coverage (if allowed in your state), which will cover your car if it's stolen or damaged while in storage, or reduce your liability limits and raise your deductibles as high as they'll go and see if you can get a low-mileage discount while you're gone. If you sell your car, buy a nonowner policy, which will cover you if you borrow or rent a car, and can make it easier to start up new coverage when you start driving your own car again.

CHAPTER 5

LIFE INSURANCE

■ ■ ■

If anyone depends on you financially, then you need life insurance. Otherwise, your family may have a tough time paying the bills without your income if anything happens to you. Having life insurance is one of the best ways to protect the financial plan that you've spent years to build.

The unfortunate truth is that most people have too little life insurance. Any coverage you have through work usually isn't enough and disappears when you leave your job. You need to buy a policy on your own, and now is a great time to do it. Prices are extraordinarily low, and even if you already have life insurance, you may be able to find a much better deal by shopping around now.

While the prices for every other type of insurance continue to rise, life insurance rates have plummeted over the past decade—the rates for the healthiest people have cut in half and continue to fall. In 1994, a healthy 40-year-old man would have had to pay at least $995 for a term insurance policy with a $500,000 death benefit that locked in the same rate for 20 years. Now, a 40-year-old man can purchase that same policy for as little as $365. If you bought a life insurance policy a few years ago, you may be able to lower your premiums and lock in the same rate for a longer time period even though you're now older, and even if you were rejected in the past because of your health, you may finally be able to find a policy at an affordable price.

Despite these great deals, people tend to make big mistakes when buying life insurance. They don't buy enough, buy the wrong kind of coverage, purchase coverage they don't need, or pay too much for a policy—sometimes getting bad advice from an agent who is trying to earn a fat commission. Fortunately, there are easy solutions to all of those problems. Online tools make it a lot simpler to calculate your insurance needs and shop for life insurance. They can also help you shut down any agents who are trying to sell you an overpriced policy you don't need. If you know how to make the most of these resources, then you can find an amazing deal on life insurance while taking some very important steps to protect your family.

Life insurance rates have dropped so much that many people can cut their costs even if they just bought a policy a few years ago.

If only health insurance could be this way . . . While the price of every other kind of insurance continues to increase every year—often at a record pace—term life insurance prices have been dropping sharply. In 1994, the lowest price for a 40-year-old man buying a $500,000 20-year term policy was $995, says Byron Udell, CEO of insurance brokerage AccuQuote. It was $465 in 2000, $365 in 2005, and the rates continue to fall.

A healthy 35-year-old man can now get a 20-year policy for as little as $275 per year. A healthy 35-year-old woman can pay even less—as little as $245 per year—because women have longer life expectancies.

Part of the reason for the big price drop is because both men and women are living longer. Thanks to medical advances, fewer people are likely to die before their insurance term is up. Meanwhile, regulators recently updated their mortality tables for the first time in more than 20 years to account for these increased life expectancies and now require insurers to set less money aside in reserves to pay potential claims, allowing them to cut rates even further.

Competition has made a big difference, too. Now that you can compare rates from the top companies within seconds online, it's easy to see who offers the best deal. In these price wars, a $10 difference in premium can lead to a big drop off in sales.

Moreover, insurers are doing a better job of assessing risks. In the past, insurers generally had four rates: male smoker and nonsmoker and female smoker and nonsmoker. Now they can have five or six rate classes for both men and women, using advanced computing capabilities to set premiums based on detailed information about your cholesterol levels, blood pressure, driving record, height and weight, as well as you and your family's medical history and other factors that might affect your odds of dying before your policy term is up. The healthiest people who qualify for a company's super-preferred rate have seen the biggest drop in prices over the past few years and can get incredibly low rates right now.

One big caveat if you're switching policies to lower your rates: Do not drop your old policy before the new one is issued. It usually takes several weeks, and a basic medical exam, to set the exact price and for the policy to take effect.

Longer-term policies are the best deal. Doubling your premium guarantee from 10 years to 20 years may only add $10 to your annual cost.

There are two types of life insurance: term and cash value. With term insurance, you only buy coverage for a certain time period, such as 10, 20, or 30 years. These policies are perfect for people who only need insurance until their kids graduate from college, until they pay off their mortgage, or until they retire and their spouse can get pension death benefits. Those are the reasons why most people buy life insurance.

Cash value policies tend to cost a lot more than term insurance—premiums are often 10 times higher—but some of the money pays for insurance and some goes into an investment account. These types of policies can be worthwhile for people who need insurance for more than 30 years, which is discussed in more detail at the end of this chapter, but term insurance is the best deal for most people because it's an incredibly inexpensive way to protect your family for as long as they need the coverage.

Term policies have changed a lot in the past few years. If you haven't shopped for insurance in ten years or so, the types of policies—in addition to the prices—may surprise you. Most term policies used to be an annually renewable term, which meant that insurers could raise your rate every year. Now you can lock in your term rate for 10, 20, or 30 years, instead, so you'll know exactly how much you'll be paying for as long as you need the policy, and the insurer is prohibited from raising your rate during that time period.

It's generally best to go with a 20- or 30-year term policy—even if you only need the coverage for ten years or so—because the extra cost is so small. A healthy 35-year-old man could pay as little as $265 per year for a $500,000 policy that locks in the same rate for ten years, but he'd only pay $275 for a 20-year term policy—just $10 more annually for ten extra years of coverage. Interestingly, because 20-year term policies are the most popular, that's where many insurers are focusing their competitive efforts. The lowest rates tend to beat even the 15-year level term policies, which cost $345 or more for a shorter guarantee. (See Figure 5.1.)

The price difference is a bit more for 30-year level term policies, but is worthwhile if it looks like there's any chance that you could need the insurance for that long—if, for example, you may still be supporting your children after college or graduate school, or if you want the coverage to last until you retire or finish paying off a 30-year mortgage. That 35-year-old man could pay as little as $540 per year for a 30-year level term policy.

You want to pick the term period carefully, because the price can jump significantly if you still need coverage after those 20 or 30 years are up. Some companies, however, let you convert to a cash value policy, which you can keep for the rest of your life. Still, for many people, 30 years is plenty of time.

FIGURE 5.1 Prices for Various Policy Terms

It's generally most cost-effective to buy a policy that locks in the same rates for 20 or 30 years, depending on how long you'll need the coverage, rather than opting for a shorter guarantee. Here are examples of the best prices for a very healthy 35-year-old man buying a $500,000 term policy:

Length of Term	Annual Premium
10-year level term	$265
15-year level term	$345
20-year level term	$275
25-year level term	$440
30-year level term	$540

Source: Insure.com

There's a huge range in prices, but it's very easy to shop around. Some Web sites, however, give you inaccurate prices.

Another group of people who can save big money on their life insurance are those who didn't shop around when they bought their policies. If you picked a policy just because you already have auto or homeowners insurance with that same company, or because an agent told you it was a good deal, you might be paying a lot more than you need to. Some companies offer much more competitive term insurance rates than others. Even though that 35-year-old man could pay as little as $275 per year for his 20-year $500,000 term policy, not all companies choose to compete by price. Some well-known companies charge at least $390 for their lowest-cost policy. Others charge more than $400.

The same is true for a 45-year-old man. He could pay as little as $695 for a 20-year $500,000 policy, but the lowest rate at some well-known companies is more than $820 per year. If you bought life insurance a few years ago and didn't shop around then, your savings can be even greater. It's easy to shop on the Web for price quotes from dozens of insurers, where you can compare costs quickly and anonymously.

However, you need to work with a Web site that asks a lot of questions about your medical history, hobbies, and other information that can affect the pricing. Unfortunately, many life insurance quote sites don't ask enough questions to provide you with accurate rates, leaving you frustrated and with higher premiums than you were expecting.

This is especially important now that it's getting tougher to qualify for the lowest rates. You need to have exceptional health, a spotless driving record, and absolutely no risky hobbies or travels in order to qualify. To get that $275 rate, for example, you must meet the following conditions:

- You must not have used any nicotine products in the past five years.
- You must have no history of cancer, heart disease, or any cardiac-related condition in any parent or sibling before age 60.
- Your cholesterol must be 210 or lower (or 220 with a cholesterol/HDL ratio of 3.5 or less) and cannot currently be controlled by cholesterol medication (but could have prior treatment for cholesterol).
- Your blood pressure must not exceed 140/85 and you cannot currently receive treatment for elevated blood pressure.
- You must meet height/weight requirements (a maximum weight of 198 pounds for a six-foot-tall man, for example).
- You must have no driving under the influence or reckless driving convictions in the past five years.
- You must have no more than one moving violation in the past three years.
- You must have no hazardous activities or occupations, such as hang gliding or scuba diving, in the past three years.
- You cannot be an active-duty military member or a bartender.

- You cannot plan to travel to India, the Philippines, Thailand, or any country currently on the U.S. State Department's Travel Warnings list.
- You cannot have a history of certain medical conditions on a long list ranging from cancer (except basal cell skin cancer) and diabetes to sleep apnea and ulcerative colitis.

Those are pretty tough standards. That company's second-lowest rate is $365 per year—nearly $100 more—but each insurance company has different criteria for getting the best rates, and if you don't make the cut for one insurer's best price, you may qualify for another company's policy that costs less than the next rate class with the first company.

A word of caution, if the quote site doesn't ask for enough information up front to provide accurate rates, then you won't find this out until after you filed an application and taken a medical exam, and by that time, you've probably invested too much time and effort to want to start your search again. Too many people end up staying with the original company even though they're paying higher rates than they could get somewhere else, because they don't want to start the process all over again.

Fortunately, there are several Web sites that ask enough questions to match you with an accurate rate. Some of the best are *www.Insure.com, www.Accuquote.com,* and *www.InsWeb.com.* The Insure.com Web site is particularly good in this area because it's the only site that lists the insurers' criteria for qualifying for each rate. You can see right away whether you're likely to receive it or not.

Keep in mind that part of the responsibility depends on you. You'll only get accurate rates if you know your cholesterol level, blood pressure, accurate height and weight, family medical history, and other details when you sit down to get quotes. Insurers won't offer you the final rate until after they check your medical records and give you a brief medical exam, so the closer your answers are to the ones they find out on their own, the more accurate your quote is likely to be.

The quote services also show you the insurers' financial-strength ratings, which is very important to consider when you're buying life insurance. Because the policy may not pay out for 20 or 30 years, you need to make sure the insurer will still be around to pay your heirs. It's generally worth a few extra dollars to avoid companies with low financial-strength ratings. Fortunately, many of the insurers offering the most competitive prices right now are massive companies with strong ratings rather than small, unknown insurers. Ratings by A.M. Best are most common, but you can also get financial-strength ratings from Fitch, Moody's, Standard & Poor's, and Weiss. Weiss Ratings (*www.weissratings.com*), which has some of the toughest standards, also has a helpful list of its highest-rated and lowest-rated companies at its Web site.

People with health problems should shop around again. They may get a lower rate or finally find coverage if they were rejected in the past.

Medical advances that have improved life expectancy, as well as insurers' improvements in assessing these risks, are making it easier for people with health problems to qualify for life insurance. Some who were rejected in the past can now get coverage, often at decent rates.

If you have diabetes, asthma, heart disease, or hepatitis C, now is a great time to shop around again for life insurance. Instead of automatically rejecting people with these conditions or grouping them all into one category, insurers are now looking at their medical conditions in a lot more detail—giving them credit, for example, if they're on certain medications and are doing a good job of controlling their condition.

Some companies, for example, have lowered rates for people with certain forms of diabetes, particularly if they aren't insulin dependent and the condition is controlled by diet or oral medications.

People with prostate cancer can get a better rate if they have certain Gleason and PSA scores, two measurements of the cancer's severity. Some insurers will offer cancer survivors standard rates if three or five years have passed since their last treatment. The Hartford recently started offering women age 40 and older who have been treated for early stages of breast cancer the same prices as other women their age.

The prices for people with medical conditions—and rules for acceptance—can still vary significantly from company to company. Some have done the research to determine a spectrum of different risks among people with similar diseases, assessing, for example, how taking certain steps can minimize your risk of dying earlier, but others may still charge everyone with the disease a high rate. Some that tout standard term rates for people with certain conditions may charge higher prices for everyone to begin with. It's essential to shop around.

Because of these variations, it's better for people with medical conditions or other insurance risks to get personalized attention rather than just searching for quotes online. Call the agents at one of the quote sites (like AccuQuote) or talk to a broker in your area who works with many companies and knows from experience which ones generally offer the best deals for people with your condition. A good broker may know the underwriters at the companies and can call with questions about their coverage rules and prescreen companies that are likely to turn you down, helping you avoid a rejection letter that may make it more difficult to get coverage elsewhere. In addition, they'll know about extra steps that can help support your case— such as providing detailed information from your doctor about your condition and how well you've controlled it—which will distinguish you from other people with similar diseases. You'll pay the same price through a broker as you will by buying the policy online, and may get an even better rate if the broker can help you qualify for a better rate class.

Also check out specialized companies. USAA is generally best if you're in the military, for example, because you can get a policy without a war exclusion, but you need to contact the company directly (*https://www.usaa.com*).

It should go without saying, but never lie on an insurance application. Insurance companies do check your medical records and generally send a nurse out to take blood and conduct other basic tests. Then they share that information with other insurers through the Medical Information Bureau, which reports medical conditions that the insurer found when underwriting your application.

If the insurer finds out that you were lying when you apply, rejection will be more likely because they'll wonder what else you left out. It's even worse if the insurance company doesn't discover your lie until after you die. At that point, they may be able to void the entire policy, leaving your family without any death benefit. It's a good idea to check your MIB record and make sure it doesn't contain any errors. Contact the MIB at *www.mib.com* or 866-692-6901. The MIB will only have a record for you if you've applied for life, health, or disability insurance within the past seven years.

Shop again for life insurance if you've lost weight, stopped smoking, lowered your cholesterol, or improved your driving record. You could lower your rate significantly.

Shedding a few pounds or a few points from your cholesterol level can make a big difference in your rate. Most insurance companies require a cholesterol level of 240 or less to qualify for their best rate; some won't offer the deepest discounts unless your cholesterol is below 220. They also have strict blood pressure and height/weight requirements. If you've improved any of these readings, you might qualify for a lower rate. Your insurer won't automatically change your rate; you need to bring it to the insurance company's attention. Also because each insurer has different cut-offs, another insurer might give you more credit for the improvement than you'll get with your current company. It's a good idea to shop around again and see who will offer you the best deal.

Quitting smoking can reduce your rate significantly, but insurers want to reduce the odds that you'll start back up again and generally want you to be nicotine-free for at least a year before giving you a lower rate. Five years off cigarettes may qualify you for a deeper discount. You need to notify your insurer—or shop around for a policy again—or else you won't get any credit for quitting.

The same is true for your driving record. Some insurers won't give you the lowest rate if you've had one or two moving violations in the past three years, but after that time has passed you may be able to cut your costs.

Knowing about these rules can help you lower your rate, but don't let any of these problems prevent you from applying for insurance now if you need the coverage. Paying a few hundred dollars extra in premiums for a year or two is much better than waiting until your condition improves to buy a policy—and running the risk that your family would end up with no coverage if anything happened to you during that time. You can always switch to a lower-cost policy later.

Making the most of a few simple cost-saving strategies can shave a few extra dollars off your premiums.

A few quick and easy strategies can cut your rates by a few extra dollars.

Buying right before your birthday—or your half birthday—may result in lower premiums for the next 20 or 30 years. Insurance prices are based on age; the older you are, the higher your rate. Every year you wait can make a difference in the cost, especially after age 40. In late 2005, the lowest rate for a 20-year $500,000 term policy was about $365 for a very healthy 40-year-old, $405 for a 41-year-old, $460 for a 42-year-old, $520 for a 43-year-old, $585 for a 44-year-old, and $650 for a 45-year-old, says Byron Udell, CEO of insurance brokerage AccuQuote. Some companies use your birthday as the cut-off; some use your nearest birthday, raising the rate at your half-birthday instead. There's no sense in buying a policy before you need it just to get the lower rate, but if you need the insurance anyway, some careful timing can save you money (see Figure 5.2).

FIGURE 5.2 How Age Affects Rates

If you buy a 20-year term policy, the price cannot rise after you purchase the policy, but the rate can increase a lot for every year you wait to buy coverage, especially as you get older. There's no reason to buy a policy before you need it, but buying before your birthday (or half-birthday) can make a difference in the long-term cost. Here are the best rates for a man buying a $500,000 20-year term policy at various ages.

Age You Buy the Policy	Annual Premiums for 20 Years
34	$265
35	$265
36	$275
37	$290
38	$310
39	$335
40	$365
41	$405
42	$460
43	$520
44	$585
45	$650
46	$715
47	$790
48	$855

Source: AccuQuote

Consider key price points when selecting the amounts. Companies typically lower rates at $250,000, $500,000, and $1 million. Round up to one of those amounts and see how much it will cost. You may be able to get $50,000 in extra coverage for very little money.

You'll usually get a discount for paying your premiums in a lump once per year rather than monthly, and may get a bigger discount if you pay through automatic debit because the insurer saves on the administrative costs of mailing you a bill.

Your employer's life insurance generally is not the best deal.

If your employer pays for your life insurance as an employee benefit, that's a good start—free insurance is definitely a good thing—but it usually isn't enough. Employers generally provide one or two times your annual income in life insurance, which is much less than most families need (most need eight to ten times your income—see below for more information on calculating the amount). In addition, if you leave your job, you lose that coverage. You'll generally need to buy more insurance.

Some employers offer additional coverage that you buy yourself and can keep after you leave the job. However, if you're healthy, you may be able to find a better deal on your own.

When insurers offer these "voluntary enrollment" policies, they generally ask few or no questions about your health and assume a certain number of unhealthy people will sign up, which boosts the prices for everyone. As a result, healthy people can save a lot of money by buying the policies on their own, where they're given credit for their good health. An individual policy asking about your medical condition, family history, risky hobbies, and generally requiring you to take a quick medical exam, may cost a healthy person as much as 50 percent less than a group life insurance policy.

Check both options and compare the costs. If you're unhealthy, on the other hand, a group health policy may provide coverage you might not qualify for on your own.

Don't buy mortgage life insurance—unless you have health problems.

Many mortgage companies offer special life insurance policies that pay off your loan if you die, so your heirs aren't stuck with the bills. The concept may sound good, but it's generally better to buy a life insurance policy on your own. You may get more coverage at a better rate and, most important, your family will be able to use the death benefit for whatever they want, not just to pay off the mortgage. If you have a low-rate mortgage, they may not need to be in any rush to pay off the loan and may have many other priorities for the money. Buying a regular term insurance policy gives them that option.

Mortgage life insurance rates also tend to be higher because you generally aren't given credit for your good health However, the reverse is true, too—if you have any health problems and are having trouble qualifying for an individual policy, you may still be able to get mortgage life insurance, which can provide your family with some coverage that you couldn't get otherwise.

Return of premium policies are popular and can give you back tens of thousands of dollars. But they aren't the best investment.

One of the best-selling new versions of term insurance returns all of your premiums if you're still alive when the term is up. Your annual premiums will be higher, but you'll get a lump sum of money after 20 or 30 years, which can come in handy to help pay college bills if you buy the policy when your kids are young, or can give you a big check when you're about to retire.

Your annual premiums are a lot more for a 20-year return of premium policy than they are for a regular 20-year term policy—a 41-year-old man could pay about $405 for a regular policy with a $500,000 death benefit, or about $1,330 for a return-of-premium policy. However, the return of premium policy will give you back all $26,600 that you've paid in premiums through the years if you're still alive in 20 years, and the amount is guaranteed.

This type of policy can help people feel better if they don't like the idea of paying premiums for years but getting nothing if they're still alive when the term is up. It is also a sneaky way to force yourself to save money, because you'll get a bill for the premiums every year. It isn't a great investment, though. If you bought a regular term policy instead and invested the price difference yourself, your investments would only need to return about 2.8 percent per year to exceed the money you'll get back from the return of premium policy. That's easy to do over 20 years.

The investment value is better if you buy a 30-year return of premium policy, because the premium difference isn't as large. A healthy 41-year-old man could pay about $930 for a regular 30-year $500,000 term policy, or $1,425 for a return of premium version. If he invested the $495 price difference himself, his investments would have to return at least 6.2 percent per year to accumulate more than the nearly $43,000 he'd get in returned premiums. The price difference tends to be even smaller for younger buyers.

If you drop a return of premium policy before the term is up, you may still get some of your premiums back, but those amounts can vary a lot from company to company. Some give back 60 percent of the premiums you've paid so far if you drop a 30-year policy after 15 years, for example. You'll still do much better if you hold it for the entire policy term.

Most people have too little life insurance, and basic rules of thumb can lead you astray. It costs very little to increase your coverage by hundreds of thousands of dollars.

Just buying life insurance isn't enough to protect your family's finances. You need to get the right amount. Too many people don't buy enough life insurance and don't realize how inexpensive it is to boost their coverage.

The key is to have enough insurance to help support your family without your income. The standard rule of thumb is to buy eight to ten times your income. That can give you a good head start, but could still leave you with too little coverage. If you're the sole breadwinner with several young children, you'll need a lot more coverage than someone who earns the same annual salary but has a spouse who also works, older children, a smaller mortgage, and a good start on college savings. Even a parent who stays at home with the children still needs insurance to pay for childcare if they were to die—even though they aren't earning an income.

To get a more accurate figure, you need to add up your family's expenses, subtract the amount of income that will continue to come in after you die, then buy enough life insurance to fill in the gap, considering your investment returns and inflation. Many online calculators can help you do the math.

You may, however, get very different answers depending on which calculator you use. Some assume that you'll want to leave enough money to pay off your house in a lump sum, in addition to covering other expenses, but if you have a low-interest mortgage, there may be no big rush to pay the remaining balance. A few calculators, like the one on Kiplinger.com's insurance page, let you choose which expenses to include.

When calculating the amount, keep in mind that you can actually buy that much coverage without having to adjust your calculation for taxes—your heirs won't pay income taxes on life insurance death benefits.

There's no reason to skimp on your coverage amount because it costs very little to increase your coverage by hundreds of thousands of dollars. If you aren't sure exactly how much you need, then just round up. That 35-year-old man in Chicago would pay $243 per year for a 20-year level term policy providing $250,000 of coverage, but it would only cost him an extra $30 per year (an annual premium of $275) to boost his coverage to $500,000. He could even increase his coverage to $1 million for only $480 per year.

Review your insurance coverage every few years. You may need to increase the amount if you get a higher-paying job, bigger mortgage, or have more income. If prices continue to drop, you may be able to lower your premiums or lock in a longer rate guarantee just by switching to another company. Also make sure your beneficiary designations are up to date, especially if you have a child, or get married or divorced.

Some people don't need life insurance at all.

Life insurance can be essential to protect your financial plans, but many people are talked into buying life insurance they don't need. The rules are simple: You only need life insurance if somebody else is depending on you financially. Parents supporting young children generally all need life insurance, whether you're earning an income or you're a stay-at-home parent. You also need life insurance if your spouse is depending on your income to help pay the bills, even if you don't have kids at home. You need life insurance if you own a business and someone needs the money to buy out your heirs if you die, or your spouse is depending on your pension but the benefits stop after you die.

Most single people and children don't need life insurance. While it can seem like a compelling argument to buy the coverage now in case your child ends up getting a medical condition that makes it tougher to qualify for coverage later, in reality very few young people get rejected for coverage because of their health. An agent might try to sell you life insurance as an investment, but there are a lot of better places where you should be investing first (see below).

You should only consider cash value life insurance if you need the coverage for more than 30 years.

As previously mentioned, there are two types of life insurance: term and cash value. Term insurance only provides coverage for a certain time period and generally doesn't pay out anything if you die before then. This insurance is the best deal for most people, who generally only need coverage for 20 or 30 years, which is the perfect amount of time if you're buying coverage until you pay off a house or until your kids grow up.

Cash value life insurance, on the other hand, is the only type of coverage that guarantees that your insurance policy will continue for the rest of your life, no matter how long you live. That long-term protection can be helpful if you need the coverage to pay potential estate-tax bills, provide for a special-needs child who won't ever be able to support himself, or provide your spouse with money if you don't have spousal pension benefits and the payments stop completely when you die. If you need insurance for more than 30 years, then you should consider a cash value life insurance policy.

Don't buy life insurance primarily as an investment. There are better ways to save.

Too many people who don't need life insurance get talked into buying a cash value policy because of its investment value. This is a lousy way to save if you don't need insurance. Even if you do need the coverage, there are generally a lot of better ways to build your savings.

Cash value life insurance includes both life insurance coverage and an investment account. The premiums are much higher than they are for term insurance—sometimes ten times as high. Some of the money goes into the investment account (called the "cash value") and some pays for the insurance coverage. You can borrow from the policy at any time (which temporarily reduces your death benefit, until you pay off the loan) or you can drop the policy and keep the cash value.

It can take quite a while to build any cash value in the policy, however. Most of these policies have high up-front fees—generally sales commissions paid to agents—that eat up a lot of the cash value in the early years. It's not unusual for a policy sold by a commissioned agent to have no cash value in the first few years, and can take ten years before your cash value equals the amount of money you've paid in premiums.

Some of this money pays for insurance, but even just the insurance portion tends to be a lot more expensive than it is for term insurance, especially in the younger years. If you can't afford to buy the coverage amount that you need, then you should switch to a term insurance policy rather than lower your coverage amount with a cash value policy. If you were to die, having the right amount of coverage will be a lot more important to your family, which is the most important reason for buying life insurance.

There are three main types of cash value policies: variable universal life, universal life, and whole life, with a savings account portion of the policy in either mutual fund-like accounts or fixed-income investments (see Figure 5.3 on the next page).

Cash value policies do have some tax advantages: the money grows in the account without any tax bill through time, and you can borrow a lot of it without owing taxes. If you do cash out the policy and take the money, you only owe taxes on the difference between the amount you've paid in premiums (which includes your money for investments and insurance) and the amount you cash out—making the tax bill a lot smaller than many people expect.

There are several ways to invest and get even bigger tax benefits, however, such as by maxing out your 401(k) at work and your Roth

FIGURE 5.3 Three Kinds of Cash Value Insurance

---

1. *Variable universal life insurance*—The part of your premium that doesn't pay for insurance is invested in mutual fund-like accounts, which you select from a handful of choices. You can decide how much money to pay in premiums, within a certain range. The more you invest, the more goes toward the cash value. Alternatively, you can keep your premiums low and use the policy primarily for the life insurance, rather than focusing on the investment account. You have the opportunity for stock-market gains in the account, but losses can eat your account alive, which happened to many people in the early 2000s. If their accounts lost too much money, they had to increase their premiums or the policies could lapse, which led to lawsuits from people whose agents didn't explain this risk.

2. *Universal life*—The insurance company does the investing for you, in bond-like investments, and your cash value moves with the bond returns. These policies had similar problems in the early 2000s. When interest rates declined, cash values dropped and some policies were on the verge of lapsing. With universal life, you can also decide how much money you want to pay in premiums. You can either pay a minimum amount, primarily to cover the life insurance costs and other expenses, or you can pay a higher amount so you can send more money to the policy's cash value (although tax laws do limit the maximum you can pay).

3. *Whole life*—This is the oldest type of cash value life insurance. You pay a fixed annual premium for the life of the policy and the insurance company invests the extra money, generally in fixed-income investments. You cannot adjust your premium amounts, but you're also guaranteed that the premiums will never increase regardless of the insurer's investment returns.

IRA. Now that capital-gains taxes are so low—15 percent for most people—you can also keep your tax bill low by buying and holding stocks for the long term or investing in index funds. With those accounts, all of the money goes towards your savings, not first paying agent commissions or buying expensive life insurance.

Commissions on cash value life insurance policies can be huge. Look carefully at no-load companies—or make a tax-free exchange to one.

No wonder so many people buy cash value life insurance when they don't really need it—the agents' commissions can be huge, often 55 percent of the total premium for the first year, then 3 percent to 5 percent in renewal commissions in each of the next five to ten years. You really need to consider the source when an agent is trying to push a policy on you and it doesn't seem like the best deal. In some cases, the deal may not be good for you, but it's a great deal for the agent.

The biggest problem with many cash value life insurance policies are the commissions, which eat up most all of your cash value in the early years. If you try to drop your policy after just a few years—before all of the sales fees have been paid—you'll generally get hit with a surrender charge. These penalties start by taking 7 percent of your cash value in the early years, generally decreasing by about a point for every year you hold the policy, until they disappear entirely after about seven to ten years.

However, that is only the case for policies sold by commissioned agents. Some cash value policies are called no-load because they're generally sold directly from the company and assess much smaller sales fees. These policies tend to have no surrender penalties and your cash value starts to grow in the first year. Ameritas (*www.ameritasdirect.com*), USAA (*https://www.usaa.com*), and TIAA-CREF (*www.tiaacref.com*) are some of the best-known no-load companies.

If you have a high-fee cash value policy, you can make a tax-free exchange (called a 1035 exchange) to a lower-cost policy. You won't owe any taxes as long as you shift directly from one company's policy to the other. Be careful to do this after most of the surrender period has passed so you don't lose too much money from the penalty, which could eat up your cost savings. If you just bought a policy, you may have to wait a few years before it's cost-effective to make the move.

If you are interested in buying a cash value policy from an agent rather than a no-load company, ask your agent if he can lower his commission. Sometimes agents have the ability to take a lower commission (sometimes dropping their commission from about 55 percent to 20 percent of the first-year premium), which boosts your cash value in the early years. Sometimes they'll be interested in doing so if it's the only way they'll sell you the policy or if another agent is competing for your business.

Because commissions are so much lower for term insurance than they are for cash value policies, a no-load company may not offer you a better term insurance rate than you'd get by buying a policy through a broker who deals with the most-competitive companies. Be sure to compare rates from no-loads with the list of top insurers at *www.insure.com, www.accuqouote.com,* and *www.insweb.com.*

The cash value policy with the lowest premium is not always the cheapest. You'll need to look at the policy illustration—but also realize that these illustrations can be illusions.

It can be incredibly complicated to compare cash value life insurance policies. It's easy to compare term policies—the policy with the lowest rate is generally the cheapest, as long as you're comparing the same insurance amount and time period—but that isn't the case with cash value policies. In fact, the policy with the lowest premium may not be the least expensive at all. Because some of the money pays for insurance and some goes into the cash value, it's much more difficult to see where the money is going. The company offering the lowest premium may actually have some of the highest insurance costs and then just send less of the money to your cash value. Others may have higher premiums but lower insurance costs and may send more money to your cash value. The only way to compare these policies is to look at the list of fees and study the policy illustrations.

These illustrations show what should happen to your cash value through time, for the first ten years, for example, then every five years or so after that. However, they make certain assumptions, which are not guaranteed. Variable universal life illustrations, for example, generally show what will happen with your cash value if your investments return 0 percent, 8 percent, or 12 percent per year. Illustrations on other types of policies show the minimum guarantees and the policy performance if the interest rates and expenses continue at their current pace.

Keep in mind that these illustrations are not guarantees. You'll probably do better than the minimum, but may not keep up with the current payouts. The only way to see how your policy is doing—and where it may go in the future—is to ask for an in-force illustration every few years. When you're comparing policies in the beginning, it's most important to look at how much of the premium makes it into the cash value in the early years—an indicator of how much money fees eat up.

It's tough to find help from an unbiased life insurance expert. Your financial planner may be able to help assess your options (although find out if they receive a commission for selling a policy). Another good resource is the Consumer Federation of America's life insurance evaluation program (*www.evaluatelifeinsurance.org*), which costs $60 for the first illustration. The CFA's experts will calculate your internal rate of return in the policy and compare it to your other options. The service can be worthwhile if you're deciding whether or not to buy a particular policy or if you're interested in switching to a new policy or dropping one you already own.

There are several ways to get money out of a cash value policy, but some provide better tax advantages than others.

If you decide that you don't need the insurance anymore, then you can drop the policy and keep the cash value (minus any surrender charges). You'll owe income taxes on the difference between the money you receive, plus any loans you've taken out, and the amount you paid in.

You can tap some of the cash without a tax bill by taking a policy loan instead, but you'll have to keep paying premiums, even though the loan amount is subtracted from your death benefit. If you drop the policy before paying back the loan, you'll owe taxes on the amount of cash you get plus any loans you haven't repaid from the past, even though that money may be long gone.

Alternatively, you could take a partial withdrawal from some types of policies, if you won't need as much life insurance coverage in the future. Withdrawals up to the amount of the premiums paid are considered a return of principal and are tax-free, even though some of the money went into the cash value and some paid the insurance premiums, but the amount you withdraw permanently lowers your death benefit.

Regardless of the type of policy you choose, it's important to make sure you get the right amount of coverage, which is why you're buying life insurance in the first place. If the premiums for a cash value policy are too high, then you should switch to a term policy you can afford and keep the right amount of insurance to protect your family.

TIPS FOR GETTING THE RIGHT LIFE INSURANCE AT THE BEST PRICE

Unlike every other kind of insurance, the prices for life insurance have plummeted over the past decade. Almost everyone can cut their premiums or lock in a lower rate for a longer time period if they know how to shop around. Even people with health conditions may be able to get better coverage now. Here are some strategies to help you find the right coverage at the lowest cost:

- Shop again for life insurance now, even if you think you have a good rate. Prices continue to fall every year. Go to a Web site like *www.Insure.com, www.AccuQuote.com,* or *www.InsWeb.com,* which ask enough medical and lifestyle questions to match you with an accurate price. Buy a 20- or 30-year term policy, which is generally a much better deal than a shorter-term policy. You may get a much lower rate if you've stopped smoking, lost weight, improved your cholesterol level, or lowered your blood pressure.

- People with health problems may also be able to lower their rates now or finally get coverage if they've been rejected in the past. It's a good time to shop around again if you have diabetes, asthma, heart disease, hepatitis C, prostate cancer, or if three or five years have passed since your last cancer treatment. You may get a better rate now, depending on the severity of the disease, if you can show the insurer that you've been controlling the condition. The rates tend to vary a lot from company to company; some specialize in certain conditions while others reject anyone with the disease. Work with an agent or broker who knows which companies tend to offer the best rates for someone like you and strategies for presenting the strongest case to the insurer.

- Buying extra life insurance through your employer may not be the best deal if you're in good health, but could be a good option if you have any medical problems. Compare the cost to buying a policy on your own, where you could qualify for a preferred rate. Buying mortgage life insurance usually isn't a good deal, either, unless you have health problems. Otherwise, buy a policy on your own so your heirs can decide where the money goes, and aren't forced to spend it all to pay off the mortgage.

- Most people have way too little life insurance. The standard rule of thumb to buy eight to ten times your income can be a good start, but your actual needs can vary a lot depending on your family's bills. To get a more accurate figure, add up your family's expenses, subtract the amount of income that will continue to come in after you die, then buy enough life insurance to fill in the gap. Several calculators can help you do the math. It can be very inexpensive to boost your coverage by hundreds of thousands of dollars. You don't need any life insurance if nobody depends on you financially.

■ Term insurance is the best type of insurance for most people, who only need the coverage until their children grow up, they pay off their mortgage, or they retire and start receiving a pension with survivor's benefits. Only consider cash value life insurance if you need the coverage for more than 30 years. Otherwise, you can generally find better places to invest your money, and the fees and insurance costs tend to eat up a lot of your potential returns. You can, however, keep these policies for the rest of your life, no matter how long that is, which can be helpful if you need the money to pay an estate-tax bill, support a special-needs child who will never be on his or her own, or provide money for your spouse to live on if your pension stops entirely when you die.

■ If you are buying a cash value policy, look at no-load companies or ask your agent to lower his commission. Look carefully at the illustration when comparing policies to see how much money pays for insurance costs and fees and how much actually makes it into the cash value. Ask for a new illustration every few years to see what's been happening to your investment and your costs, and consider making a tax-free exchange to a lower-cost policy after the surrender period has passed.

CHAPTER 6

LONG-TERM CARE INSURANCE

■ ■ ■

Buying long-term care insurance can be one of the most important moves you can make to protect your retirement savings.

You think college costs are high? That's nothing compared to just one year in a nursing home, which now costs almost $75,000 per year, according to the MetLife Mature Market Institute. That's in today's dollars. If you're 55 years old now, the annual cost could top $250,000 per year by age 80, when you're more likely to need care. Those expenses can quickly wipe out the retirement savings you've taken years to build. It's even worse when one spouse needs special care while the other is still in good health—using up most of their nest egg and leaving the other spouse with very little to live on for years. That's not quite the life you were expecting when carefully saving money in your 401(k) and IRA.

The government won't help out nearly as much as many people think. Medicare provides very little coverage for long-term care expenses and Medicaid only kicks in after you've spent almost everything you own—and even then leaves you with few care choices. Who knows what's going to happen to the government assistance over the next few decades.

However, you can buy long-term care insurance to pay many of these huge expenses, giving you hundreds of dollars every day to pay for care in a nursing home, your own home, or in an assisted-living facility. The cost of a policy depends on the age when you buy it, your health, and the benefits you choose. For about $2,200 per year, a 55-year-old can get a policy that pays out a $200 daily benefit for three years, after a 60-day waiting period, and increases the benefit amount by 5 percent each year. That will give you just about enough coverage to pay the full bill even if inflation boosts the annual cost of care to $250,000 by the time you're 80.

Adult children whose parents are in a nursing home are some of the biggest advocates for long-term care insurance right now, buying policies on themselves after watching their parents' savings be destroyed and their care choices limited because of the high costs of long-term care.

The long-term care insurance business has been going through a lot of problems recently, though, with many insurers leaving the business or raising rates significantly for senior citizens who are living on a limited income. Here's how to get the right coverage and find a company that's likely to be there when you need the payout.

You can't count on the government to cover your long-term care costs.

Many people mistakenly think that Medicare will pay for their long-term care costs. They're generally wrong. It's tough to qualify for Medicare's nursing-home coverage, and the benefits are limited even if you do make the cut. Most people in nursing homes can't get Medicare to pay for their care costs, and even fewer people qualify for benefits if they receive care in their own homes.

In order to receive Medicare's nursing-home benefits, you must first spend three days in the hospital, and then the government program will only cover up to 100 days in a skilled-nursing facility. Medicare covers the full cost of the first 20 days, then you have to pay $119 per day for days 21 to 100 and Medicare will pay the additional costs. (You can buy a medigap policy to cover your $119 out-of-pocket cost—see Chapter 2 for more information.)

Medicare only provides coverage to people who are receiving skilled-nursing care, which is a tough standard to meet. Many people in nursing homes only need custodial care, not skilled care, and will have to pay the bills themselves. Then, even you do qualify for Medicare's coverage you're on your own after 100 days.

Medicare also provides very little coverage for care in your home, and no coverage for care in an assisted-living facility, which are two categories that long-term care insurance will generally pay for.

Medicaid, on the other hand, pays the bills for most people who live in a nursing home, covering the costs after you've spent nearly all of your own money. However, recipients need to make huge sacrifices to qualify for coverage, and your care choices will be severely limited just because Medicaid is paying the bills.

The rules for qualifying for Medicaid vary a lot from state to state. Generally, Medicaid will only pay your nursing-home costs after you've spent all but about $2,000 of your assets (not counting your home and car) and gives you another $2,000 to pay for your burial. In addition, you can only keep from $30 to $70 of your monthly income; the rest must be used to pay your nursing-home costs.

If you have a spouse who still lives at home (called the "community spouse"), they can keep some more money, but that amount varies a lot from state to state, allowing them to keep from about $1,500 to $2,500 in monthly income and just $18,000 to $90,000 in savings plus their house and car. That's not going to support much of a lifestyle in retirement. If you have questions about qualifying for Medicaid in your state, contact an elder-law attorney. You can find specialists in your area through the National Academy of Elder Law Attorneys (*www.naela.org*).

Your choice of care will also be limited if Medicaid is paying your bills. Some nursing homes don't accept Medicaid patients at all, or relegate them to certain wings of the facility and require them to share a room; and Medicaid generally doesn't cover home care or assisted-living facilities. You'll have a lot more flexibility if you can afford long-term care insurance instead.

You're never too rich to need long-term care insurance.

Some old rules of thumb say that you don't need long-term care insurance if you have more than $1 million in assets because you can afford to pay the bills from your own pocket.

That's a mistake.

First of all, $1 million won't get you very far at today's nursing-home prices, and will cover even less in the future. Remember, the nearly $75,000 per year in average costs today will top $250,000 in 25 years if prices continue to rise by about 5 percent per year. It's tough to imagine that even happening. Hopefully some changes will be made by then to help make the care more affordable, but you still don't want to get stuck with the possibility that you'll have to cover all of those bills yourself.

Most important, if you think you can afford potential long-term care costs, then you can definitely afford the premiums for the insurance instead. What sounds worse: $3,000 per year for insurance or more than $75,000 per year for care?

Buying long-term care insurance lets you shift some of the risk to the insurance company. You give them a set premium each year (which may go up a bit through time, but hopefully won't) and in return they cover a potentially giant, unknown expense. It's the same way that rich people still buy insurance on their health, cars, and homes even though they could afford to pay the bills themselves.

You may never end up needing long-term care, but if you know those costs are covered, you can afford to spend more money on retirement without having to worry about setting aside a big pot of money to pay for the potential expenses.

The opposite, however, is not true. If you can't afford long-term care premiums, or don't think you can keep up the payments through time, don't buy a policy. The worst move is to buy a policy, pay the premiums for years, and then have to drop it when you get older—right at the time when you're likely to need the coverage the most. If you drop the coverage before you need care, you'll get nothing in return, even if you've paid premiums for years. If you don't have much money to begin with, and understand the limitations on Medicaid coverage, at least you know that the government program can help pay some of the bills.

Ignore average nursing home costs when selecting the benefit amount. The price range can be huge depending on where you live.

The average cost of a private room in a nursing home is now $203 per day (almost $75,000 per year) throughout the United States, according to the MetLife Mature Market Institute, but the price varies enormously from city to city. The average daily cost is just $135 in Birmingham, Alabama, and up to $348 in Stamford, Connecticut. That adds up to a big difference over just one year—totaling nearly $50,000 in Birmingham or more than $125,000 in Stamford (see Figure 6.1).

The price can also vary a lot within one city. There are high-quality and lower-quality nursing homes everywhere, which can have a big difference in price. It might feel strange, but it's a good idea to contact a nursing home or two where you wouldn't mind living someday just to get an idea of how much a high-quality nursing home costs in your area.

You may want to boost your benefit amount even higher if you're interested in receiving care in your home, which most people are. The average hourly rate for a home health aide is $19, according to the MetLife Mature Market Institute. Even if you don't require 24-hour care, the cost can easily top the price tag for a nursing home. In fact, quite a few people in nursing homes may have preferred to get care in their homes, but couldn't afford the extra cost.

All good long-term care policies now provide at least as much coverage for home care as they do for nursing-home care. If you have an old policy, however, you may want to upgrade it to a newer version. Many policies purchased in the mid-1990s only covered home care at 50 percent of the rate of nursing-home care, which

FIGURE 6.1 Nursing Home Costs throughout the United States

The average rate for a private room in a nursing home costs $203 per day, or $74,095 per year, in 2005, a 5.7 percent increase over the 2004 rate. The average hourly rate for a home health aide is $19. However, average costs vary significantly from city to city, for example:

City	Average Daily Nursing Home Cost	Average Hourly Home Health Aide
Birmingham, AL	$135	$13
Los Angeles, CA	$215	$18
San Francisco, CA	$339	$21
Denver, CO	$175	$22
Stamford, CT	$348	$21
Orlando, FL	$185	$16
Chicago, IL	$159	$16
Wichita, KS	$139	$16
Boston, MA	$277	$22
Omaha, NE	$184	$20
New York City, NY	$320	$15
Syracuse, NY	$243	$18
Milwaukee, WI	$203	$23

Source: MetLife Mature Market Institute

could leave you with too little money to choose that option. If your home-care coverage isn't enough, contact your insurance company and find out how much it would cost to upgrade to a newer version. If you stay with your current company, the added cost will probably be a lot less than it would with another insurer.

Choosing a longer waiting period will lower your premiums, but could cost you big money out of pocket—especially when you consider the effects of inflation.

The longer the waiting period is before the policy starts to pay out (also called the "elimination period"), the lower your premium is. A 55-year-old would pay $2,430 per year for a John Hancock policy with a $200 daily benefit, three-year benefit period, and a 30-day waiting period. Extending the waiting period to 60 days would lower the price to $2,227; $2,025 for a 90-day waiting period; $1,822 for a 180-day waiting period; and $1,620 for a 365-day waiting period (see Figure 6.2).

Buying the long waiting period comes with a big downside: You have to pay the long-term care bills yourself for six months or a year before the insurance starts to pay out. At a daily rate of $200, that translates into $36,000 from your own pocket before the policy with the 180-day waiting period pays benefits or $73,000 for the 365-day

FIGURE 6.2 How Your Coverage Choices Affect Your Price

Annual premiums for a 55-year-old buying a $200 daily benefit from John Hancock with 5 percent compound inflation and various waiting period and benefit period options:

Waiting Period	Benefit Period				
	Two Years	Three Years	Five Years	Ten Years	Unlimited
30 days	$1,841	$2,430	$3,166	$4,050	$5,350
60 days	$1,687	$2,227	$2,902	$3,712	$4,904
90 days	$1,534	$2,025	$2,639	$3,375	$4,458
180 days	$1,381	$1,822	$2,375	$3,037	$4,013
365 days	$1,227	$1,620	$2,111	$2,700	$3,567

Source: John Hancock Life Insurance Company

waiting period—a huge payout difference just to save about $200 on your annual premium.

Moreover, that's in today's dollars. Your share of the costs becomes much worse through time.

If nursing-home costs continue to increase by about 5 percent per year, that $200 daily cost will rise to $677 in 25 years, causing you to pay more than $120,000 out of your pocket for the 180-day waiting period before you can receive benefits; or more than $245,000 for the 365-day waiting period.

Instead, it's better to go with the 30-day or 60-day waiting period, which will keep your out-of-pocket costs at a more reasonable $6,000 or $12,000 in today's dollars.

If you're trying to keep your premiums low, it's generally better to go with a shorter benefit period than a longer waiting period because you end up playing the odds. Chances are you won't need coverage for longer than three years, but no matter how long you'll need care—whether it's one year, three years, or more—you'll still get stuck paying for the waiting period out of your own pocket first.

Short and fat is better than long and lean.

The toughest decision is which benefit period to choose. You can generally have benefits pay out anywhere from two years to ten years or even get an unlimited amount of coverage. Buying a longer benefit period boosts your premiums significantly. If that 55-year-old bought the John Hancock policy with the $200 daily benefit, 60-day waiting period, and 5 percent inflation protection, a two-year benefit period would cost $1,687 per year while an unlimited benefit period costs $4,904 per year (see Figure 6.2).

That's a huge price difference, but the difference in coverage amount is even larger. If you're unfortunate enough to need care for ten years or more, a two-year benefit period will barely put a dent in your long-term care costs. You'll have hundreds of thousands of dollars in extra expenses, and probably end up on Medicaid.

However, the average nursing home stay is only 2.6 years, so it's all a matter of playing the odds. Most people choose to round up and buy a three-year benefit period, which would cost that 55-year-old $2,227 per year, and hope they don't beat the averages. Some people opt for a longer benefit period if they have a family history of Alzheimer's disease or other long-lasting medical conditions. You can reduce your costs a lot by lowering the benefit period from unlimited to ten years, which would cost $4,050, and reduce the odds significantly that you'd ever run out of coverage. A six-year benefit period would lower the costs even further, down to $2,902 per year.

Just like every other feature in long-term care insurance, it's all a matter of making tradeoffs between the cost of coverage and the amount of care you can get.

Some insurance companies, like John Hancock, are offering a new policy variation that can help people feel more comfortable with taking a shorter benefit period. This shared-care benefit lets a couple pool their benefit periods—if you each get a three-year benefit period, for example, then one spouse can use the coverage for two years while the other one still has four years of coverage left. The shared-care benefit costs a little more than getting two standard policies with the same amount of coverage (generally about 10 percent extra), but because the odds are slim that you'll both need coverage for a long time, this can help you buy a lower benefit amount and still have plenty of coverage if one spouse ends up needing several extra years of care.

If you cannot afford a lifetime benefit, it's better to get as much daily benefit as you need for a shorter time period, rather than skimping on the daily benefit but buying the policy for a longer time period. That way, you'll be totally covered for several years, which buys you and your family some time to decide what to do if your care needs last longer than your policy's coverage.

Inflation protection is essential, but don't just look at price. The cheapest type of coverage is a lot more expensive over the long run.

Buying the right amount of coverage is only the beginning. You also need to make sure you continue to have enough coverage through the years—especially because it may be decades before you need the care.

If nursing-home costs continue to rise by about 5 percent per year, the average care bill of $200 per day will increase to $677 in 25 years. If you buy long-term care insurance at age 55 and don't need care until age 80 (the age when most people start to need care) buying the right amount of coverage today could leave you with way too little money to pay your bills. Your $73,000 in benefits won't get you very far if the costs top $250,000 per year.

There are several ways you can adjust your coverage to keep up with the rising cost of care. The most common is to buy a policy with 5 percent compound inflation protection, which can help your coverage keep pace with the costs. Your $200 of daily benefit today will grow to $677 per year, which can be every important to have if costs continue to rise at their current pace. Buying this type of inflation protection can double your premiums, but it's the best way to make sure your coverage keeps up with the cost of care, especially if you buy the policy in your 50s or 60s.

Insurers generally offer simple inflation protection coverage, too, which uses simple interest, rather than compound interest, to boost your coverage amount by 5 percent each year. For the $200 policy, for example, the daily benefit will increase by just $10 per year, giving you a benefit of $450 after 25 years rather than $677.

This type of coverage is less expensive—that 55-year-old would pay $1,687 per year for the policy with the 60-day waiting period, three-year benefit period, and a $200 daily benefit that rises each year with 5 percent simple inflation, versus the $2,227 he'd pay with the 5 percent compound inflation increase. The payout difference, however, could be huge by the time he needs care, with compound-inflation policy providing more than $250,000 in annual coverage when he or she is 80, while the policy with the simple inflation would only pay out about $164,000.

The payout difference, however, is a lot smaller if you buy the policy when you're older. If you're shopping for a policy at age 70, for example, opting for simple rather than compound inflation protection can make the coverage a lot more affordable and won't make as much of a difference over a shorter time period. If you're having a tough time paying for your long-term care insurance when you get older, switching to simple inflation protection can be a good way to lower your costs without changing your coverage all that much.

Because of the high price of inflation protection, however, many insurers now offer another option for dealing with the rising cost of care. Instead of buying the inflation protection up front, which automatically increases your daily benefit every year, they let you decide whether or not to increase your benefit amount in the future, generally letting you boost the coverage every two or three years. A policy with these "future purchase options" costs a lot less than the compound inflation protection—$911 per year for the 55-year-old with the $200 daily benefit versus the $2,227 he or she is paying for the 5 percent compound inflation adjustment. Because of the price difference, a lot of insurers offering group policies are now offering this type of inflation protection, and it is attractive to people who worry that the cost of care may not continue to increase at as fast a pace in the future.

Keep in mind that choosing this option may actually be a lot more expensive in the future. When you buy the future purchase options, your benefit amount doesn't automatically change—leaving you with $200 per day, for example, unless you take action to increase it—and when you do add the extra coverage amount, the price is based on your age when you boost the coverage, not the age when you originally purchased the policy. Because the cost of long-term care insurance increases significantly as you get older, boosting your coverage amount through time can become incredibly expensive.

A study by Legacy Services Inc., an independent insurance agency that specializes in long-term care insurance programs for large employers, did a study that illustrates the cost difference. A 45-year-old can buy a policy with a $120 daily benefit, three-year benefit period, 90-day waiting period, and 5 percent compound inflation protection for $560 per year. By the time he or she reaches age 65, the daily benefit will rise to $317, but the cost will remain the same—$560 per year. Meanwhile, the person buying future purchase options will be paying $979 per year for the same coverage amount. The price difference is even greater at age 80, when the person with the automatic inflation adjustment will have $658 per day in coverage and still pay $560 per year in premiums, while the person with future purchase options will end up paying about $5,371 per year to have the same daily benefit.

Because of the pricing structure for future purchase options, the cost rises the most at exactly the time when it gets tougher to pay for the increases—when you're in your 70s, have been retired for years, and are living on a limited income. You can always choose not to boost your coverage after a certain point, which can keep your premiums more affordable and may work out fine if the cost of care doesn't rise as quickly in the future. However, if costs continue rising at their current pace, then you could fall short of your needs. It's a risk you need to assess when deciding whether or not it's worth the extra premium to get inflation worries out of the way in the beginning.

Before buying a policy with future purchase options, compare the cost through time with a policy that automatically adjusts your coverage for inflation. People who buy the policies at a young age will see the biggest difference in costs through time.

The younger you are when you buy the policy, the lower your premiums. But you'll end up paying for many more years.

Another huge question is when to buy the policy. A few years ago, the average age was in the low 70s, but people are now buying policies a lot earlier. The average buyer is in the high 50s for individual policies and high 40s for group policies offered by employers.

The age has dropped, in part, because people are starting to buy the coverage as part of their retirement planning, and because they've noticed the price difference. The younger you are when you buy the policy, the lower your annual premiums will be. That policy with the $200-daily benefit, three-year benefit period, 60-day waiting period, and 5 percent compound inflation protection would cost $1,824 per year if you buy it at age 45, $2,227 if you buy it at age 55, and $3,427 if you buy it at age 65. Buying earlier looks like a great deal, but you do end up paying premiums for many more years before you're likely to need coverage. On the flip side, if you wait to buy the policy when you're older, you'll need to buy a much bigger daily benefit to keep up with the cost of care (and the amount your benefit would have grown to if you had the 5 percent compound inflation protection). Moreover, the older you are when you buy the policy; the chances are greater that you'll develop a medical condition that makes it tougher to qualify for coverage or for the insurer's best rates.

It's generally best to buy the policy in your 50s or 60s, or earlier if you can afford it, but before then, you're likely to have other more-pressing priorities. At that age, your first priority is to save for college and retirement, and it's important to make sure you have enough life, health, and disability insurance to protect your family. As you free up more cash, however—after your kids graduate from college, for example—it's a perfect time to start looking at long-term care insurance. If your employer offers a group policy at work, you may want to consider buying coverage even earlier; especially if you're offered a group discount or if you're in poor health and can get coverage that you might not qualify for on your own.

Even if your employer offers long-term care insurance, you may find a better deal on your own.

More employers are starting to offer long-term care insurance to their employees. You generally pay the premiums yourself, but you may get a group discount and it may be easier for someone in poor health to qualify for coverage. It's worthwhile to check out the coverage and prices.

It's also important to compare the cost to buying a policy on your own. Each employer's plan is very different. Some may offer a group discount, but other discounts they don't offer may offset that price cut—some don't offer a spousal discount, for example, which can lower your premiums by 20 percent or more. Also check how the benefits are adjusted for inflation. As previously mentioned, many group plans offer inflation protection through future purchase options, which reduces premiums substantially at first but may boost costs over the long run.

The rules for underwriting (the criteria insurers consider when determining prices, such as medical conditions) can vary a lot, too. Some group policies offer limited underwriting, which means that they ask few medical questions and almost anyone can qualify for coverage. Insurers figure that employees are a preselected group—if you're working full-time, then you're probably in reasonable health. However, if you're in particularly good health, you may get a better deal on your own, where an insurer asks detailed questions about your medical condition and can give the lowest-risk people a preferred rate.

Some employers let you buy coverage for your parents at a discount, which may be a good deal and a little easier to qualify for than buying coverage on their own.

There's no guarantee that premiums won't increase in the future, so it's important to pick your company very carefully.

Horror stories have filled the press in the past few years about long-term care insurance companies that offered lowball rates to attract customers, then jacked up the prices after seniors had paid the premiums for years—when they could afford the price increase the least. When you buy a long-term care policy, there's no guarantee that your rate won't rise. The insurer can't raise your rate after you buy a policy just because of your age or your health, but it can increase rates for whole groups of people if it can prove to regulators that the rate hike is necessary to have enough money to pay claims.

Even though many insurers have never needed to boost their rates, it's not a big surprise that some of them have because it's tough for insurance companies to assess their risks.

Because long-term care insurance is a relatively new form of insurance, insurers hadn't had a lot of experience with claims, and didn't know how much it was going to end up costing them. They misjudged what people would do with their policies, assuming a larger number would pay premiums for years then drop them before they had to pay out claims. People were a lot smarter than they were expecting, however, and kept their policies, knowing that otherwise they were throwing away money.

Even having claims experience can only help long-term care insurers so much, because medical advances continue to change the need for care. People are living longer, for example, but need care for a longer time period, too. Moreover, the type of care is also changing. Assisted-living facilities didn't really exist when the first generation of policies was introduced, and few people received care in their homes. Now those are two main reasons to buy long-term care insurance.

That's the biggest problem with long-term care insurance; an enormous amount of time can pass between when you buy the policy and when you need the coverage, and you're generally stuck with the same insurer for decades. You can always try to switch to another insurer, but by then you'll be a lot older and start with much higher premiums (losing credit for all of the years you paid premiums with the other company). In addition if you've developed a medical condition during that time, you may have a tough time even qualifying for a new policy.

Despite all of these complications, though, long-term care insurance is still about the only way to help you pay for the potentially enormous expenses if you need care. It's worthwhile to buy a policy, but you need to choose your company very carefully.

Even though some insurance companies raised their rates by 50 percent or more, a few of the big players—like John Hancock, Genworth (formerly GE Financial), and MetLife—have never had to raise rates for the policies they sold themselves (they sometimes have to boost rates for policies they bought from other companies that left the business). That's no guarantee that they won't ever need to boost rates in the future, but it's a good sign that they've made it so far without any problems. Stick with big insurers that have been in the long-term care insurance business for many years and make long-term care insurance one of their specialties (because the rate-setting strategies are totally different than they are for other types of insurance). If an insurer offers a much lower rate than its competitors, you should be suspicious. It's generally worth a little extra money up front to stick with a big insurer with a history of rate stability.

Thanks to new laws, it's less likely that insurance companies will need to raise rates in the future. The National Association of Insurance Commissioners passed a model regulation, approved by most states, that sets tougher standards for insurers when determining long-term care insurance rates and will make it much more difficult for them to get approval from regulators to raise rates for policyholders. As a result, some insurers needed to raise their rates for new customers by 20 percent or so—even higher for potentially open-ended risks like lifetime coverage—but these customers will be less likely to experience a rate increase.

No matter how carefully you pick an insurance company, though, it still can raise rates in the future. Keep that in mind when deciding how much coverage to buy. Don't stretch too far to buy coverage that you can barely afford and definitely won't be able to keep up after a rate hike. Adjust your coverage options so it's affordable up front, and set aside a little extra money just in case your rates do increase.

Another option: Some people choose to get a ten-pay policy, where they pay high premiums for ten years then never have to pay again, which can help them avoid rate increases in the future. This ties up a lot of money that you might need elsewhere in your finances, and you need to verify with the contract that the insurer cannot increase your rates in the future. The timing can work well, though, if you're buying a policy at 55 and want to be finished paying premiums by the time you retire at age 65.

If your premiums do rise, it's generally better to adjust your policy rather than buy a new one.

If your insurer does increase your premiums, you're generally in a bind. Unlike auto insurance, where you can just switch to another company, you'll have a tough time getting a good deal anywhere else—especially if you bought your policy quite a while ago. Now that you're older and your health may not be as good—and insurers are subject to stricter pricing requirements—any new insurance company is going to charge you a lot more than you were originally paying with your current insurer. In many cases, that premium is even higher than the amount you're paying after your insurer's price hike.

If your long-term care insurance company does raise your rate, it doesn't hurt to shop around and see if you can get a better deal elsewhere (although never drop your policy before getting a new one, just in case you end up having a tougher time qualifying than you expected). You're unlikely to find a better deal, though.

If you're having a tough time affording the extra premiums, you can make some changes in your current policy to help cut back on the costs. Instead of cutting back on your benefit amount, which may leave you with too little coverage to pay the bills, consider lowering your benefit period. That way, you'll still have full coverage for the first several years and the odds are unlikely that you'll need coverage longer than that. A survey of 1.6 million long-term care policies, for example, found that only 14 percent of the claims lasted longer than two years. Just 6 percent lasted longer than three years. Switching from an unlimited lifetime benefit to a three-year benefit period could lower your premiums by 35 percent to 40 percent.

Depending on your age, you could also change to a different type of inflation protection. If you're getting 5 percent compound inflation now, you'll be able to cut your rates by switching to a simple inflation adjustment. If you're older than 75, you might not need inflation protection at all anymore. Compare your current benefit amount to the cost of care in nursing homes in your area. If you have enough insurance to cover the current costs, then check how much it would cost to boost your benefit amount to account for a few years' worth of future cost increases, then eliminate inflation protection. You might come out ahead that way.

You can also cut your costs by increasing the waiting period from 30 to 60 days. You don't want to go much longer than that or else you'll end up with tens of thousands of dollars in extra out-of-pocket costs before coverage kicks in.

Even if your premiums don't increase, it's important to make sure your policy is up to date. The first generation of long-term care insurance policies weren't particularly good—they didn't cover home care or only covered it at half the rate as nursing home costs, and didn't cover assisted-living facilities at all. As the types of care change, some insurers let their current policyholders upgrade their policies (often for additional premium). The extra cost can be worth it; otherwise, you could end up without any coverage for some of the most attractive types of care.

Buying a policy for your parents may be a great investment.

If your parents can't afford a long-term care policy, consider buying one for them. The investment may be worth it. Not only can it help preserve your inheritance—leaving it to you rather than spending it all on care—but it can also protect your own nest egg. Many people may be counting on Medicaid to pay their parents' long-term care bills, which it can do once they've spent most all of their money. They change their minds, though, when they look at the care choices for their parents under Medicaid, and end up paying a big part of their parents' bills out of their own retirement savings— leaving them with tens of thousands of dollars less than they expected to have for their own retirement.

Being on Medicaid limits your choice of nursing homes (many don't accept Medicaid patients at all) and generally won't pay for a private room. It won't pay for care in your own home or in an assisted-living facility either. Buying a long-term care policy for your parents can give them many more choices. If your employer offers long-term care insurance at group rates, the offer may extend to your parents, who might be able to get a discount or qualify for coverage they couldn't get elsewhere if they have any medical conditions. Make sure all of your own bases are covered first—having the right amount of health, life, and disability insurance for your own family—but after that, think of the potential costs you may have if your parents need long-term care.

TIPS FOR GETTING THE RIGHT LONG-TERM CARE INSURANCE COVERAGE AT THE BEST PRICE

Buying long-term care insurance can be one of the best ways to protect your retirement plan, covering hundreds of thousands of dollars in potential expenses. However, you need to make some key decisions when you buy a policy, so you can find a good insurer, minimize your costs, and lower the risk of a rate increase:

- The average nursing home stay cost $203 per day in 2005, but don't just use national or state averages when choosing a benefit amount. The cost of coverage can vary significantly depending on where you live. Check out prices for facilities you'd consider in your area, and get even more coverage if you'd like to receive care in your home, which tends to cost more.

- The longer the waiting period, the lower your premiums, but you'll also need to pay more money out of your pocket before benefits kick in. Considering inflation, this could leave you paying for tens of thousands of dollars in costs before you even start to receive coverage. A 60-day waiting period is generally the best balance of premium and coverage.
- The most difficult decision is the length of the benefit period. Short benefit periods cost significantly less than unlimited coverage, but you'll run the risk of having hundreds of dollars of expenses if you have a long nursing-home stay. Because the average nursing-home stay is 2.6 years, most people round up and opt for a three-year benefit period, which is a good balance of price and coverage. Some people choose to pay extra for a longer benefit period—six years, ten years, or unlimited—if they have a family history of Alzheimer's or another long-lasting disease.
- Inflation protection is essential, especially if you're buying the policy in your 50s or 60s. A 5 percent compound inflation protection can double your premiums but generally provides the best coverage at that age. A "future purchase option," where you can choose whether or not to increase your coverage through time, costs a lot less at the beginning but tends to become a lot more expensive through time because the rates for your extra coverage are based on your older age.
- The younger you are when you buy the policy, the lower your premiums will be, but you'll also be paying for a longer time period. It's generally best to buy a policy in your 50s or 60s, after you have fewer family obligations. Consider buying a policy after you finish paying college bills, when you should have more free money for the premiums.

- There is always the risk that your premiums will rise. Stick with a big company that does a lot of long-term care business and hasn't had to raise its rates in the past.
- A group policy may not be your best option if you're healthy; also compare costs for individual policies, which may give you a spousal discount and more credit for good health.
- Consider buying a policy for your parents if they can't afford it themselves. It will expand their care options significantly and help preserve your inheritance and your own retirement savings.

CHAPTER 7

DISABILITY INSURANCE

■ ■ ■

Could you still pay your bills if you were unable to work for a long time? It's something you need to consider. One in three working Americans will become disabled for 90 days or more before age 65, missing work for an average of 2.5 years. At age 40, the average worker has a 21 percent chance of being disabled for 90 days or more before age 65, but only a 14 percent chance of dying during that time. Your family's financial toll can be even worse while you're disabled because your own expenses continue even though your income has stopped.

If you have disability insurance through work, that's a start, but that still may leave you with big gaps. Employer policies generally only cover 60 percent of your salary—excluding bonuses and commissions—and that's before the benefits are taxed. Unless you can afford to live on about half your salary, it's a good idea to get extra insurance.

Disability insurance is incredibly complicated to shop for. Each company's policy is different, and you can't just compare by price. Tiny variations in wording can make a huge difference in coverage, and it can be surprisingly difficult for some people even without risky jobs to get coverage, like doctors and writers who work at home.

The disability insurance business has gone through a tumultuous decade. Many companies lost money and left the business after paying a slew of expensive claims in the late 1980s and early 1990s.

Three of the largest disability insurers merged to become one, UnumProvident, which in 2004 received a $15 million fine after the insurance regulators in every state banded together to investigate the company's sales practices. The regulators also required the company to reevaluate 300,000 claims it denied over the past several years.

Despite these challenges, disability insurance is still the best way to protect your income if you're unable to work. You need to be careful, however. Here's how to get the right kind of coverage at the best price.

Disability insurance through work is a start, but probably isn't enough.

Many people think they have a lot more disability insurance coverage than they do. If you have insurance through your employer, that's a good start, but most group policies cover only 60 percent of an employee's income, and then the benefits are generally taxable if the employer paid the premiums. That 60 percent rarely includes commissions and bonuses, leaving many salespeople, Wall Street workers, and top executives with a lot less money than they're used to living on. Most group policies cap monthly benefits at $5,000 to $10,000, even if it's much less than 60 percent of the employee's base income—adding up to $60,000 to $120,000 per year before taxes.

If that isn't enough money to cover your bills, then you should consider getting an individual disability insurance policy to supplement your employer's coverage.

Individual disability insurance policies generally pay up to 50 to 70 percent of your income, generally up to $15,000 per month. Because of the tax rules, that's actually a lot more than you'd get from a group policy. Benefits from group disability plans are generally taxed, but the benefits aren't taxable when you buy an individual policy and pay the premiums on your own. You may be able to cover up to a total of 80 percent of your income when you use an individual policy to supplement group coverage. Individual policies are also portable—you can take them with you when you leave your job, and premiums for most policies don't increase for the rest of your life.

The premiums vary a lot based on your occupation, health, and details of your coverage, but a 40-year-old man would generally pay from $1,500 to $2,500 per year for a policy that could pay $3,000 per month as long as he's disabled, and continue for the rest of his life, or from $2,500 to $3,500 for a 40-year-old woman.

You can't just compare premiums. Coverage can vary enormously from company to company, and tiny variations in wording can make a huge difference in claims payouts.

Disability insurance is the most complicated type of insurance to shop for. Every company's policy is a bit different, so you can't just compare price. It also has its own language, with terms such as non-cancelable and guaranteed renewable, own-occupation, elimination period, and residual benefits, which can make a giant difference in the payout amount.

The most important thing to look for is the policy's definition of disability, which determines whether or not your claim will be paid. Social Security, for example, has one of the most restrictive definitions of disability, only paying out if the disability is expected to last for at least 12 months and you cannot do any kind of job.

On the opposite end, some policies, called "own-occupation coverage," pay out full benefits if you cannot do your old job anymore, even if you end up making as much money in a new job. This type of coverage is particularly valuable for people in physical, highly skilled areas, such as surgeons, who may be unable to do their job if they hurt their hands and are unlikely to find another job that pays nearly as much. Only a few companies, such as Berkshire Life, Standard of Oregon, and MetLife, offer pure own-occupation coverage until age 65, and the coverage is limited for many kinds of doctors.

Most insurance companies now provide own-occupation coverage for the first two to five years, and then switch to "any-occupation coverage," only paying full benefits if you're unable to work in your own occupation and are not working in another job. Some stop paying entirely if you go back to work anywhere else; others become a "loss of income" policy and only pay benefits based on the percentage of the income you lost. If you do go back to work and earn more than 20 percent of your former salary, for example, then the benefits are reduced based on the amount you're earning from your new job. If your new job only pays half as much as your old job, then you'll get 50 percent of your monthly benefit. There are also several other key phrases to look for, which can make a big difference in your coverage (see Figure 7.1).

FIGURE 7.1 Disability Insurance Definitions

The policy's definition of total disability is the most important thing to look for, which will make a huge difference in whether or not your policy will pay out, but a few other key phrases will also affect your coverage. Look for policies that include the following:

- *Noncancelable and guaranteed renewable* means that the insurance company cannot drop you or raise your rates over time. Just being *guaranteed renewable* but not noncancelable is a big difference; in that case, your insurer can raise your rate.
- *Cost-of-living adjustment (COLA)* increases your benefits to keep up with inflation, just as your salary would rise through time. It's either based on the Consumer Price Index or adjusted by a set amount each year (generally from 4 percent to 10 percent). Dropping this option entirely can cut your premiums by 25 percent but may leave you with too little coverage.
- *Elimination period* is the waiting period before benefits kick in, generally from 30 to 90 days. The shorter the waiting period is, the higher your premium. When choosing the time period, consider how many sick days you have and any coverage from your employer's plan, and how long you can afford to pay the bills from your savings without too much strain.
- *Residual benefits* pay out for partial disability—if you need to cut back from a full-time to a part-time job. It pays partial benefits based on your loss of income and doesn't require you to be totally disabled first.

Because disability insurance is so complicated and has its own language, it's best to work with a broker who specializes in disability insurance, works with many companies, and knows which ones tend to offer the best coverage for someone like you. Some strong companies, like Northwestern Mutual, only sell through their own agents, which might be good to contact, too. You may also get a good deal if your employer lets you buy extra coverage on your own at a discount, in addition to the group coverage you get for free.

Your occupation can make a huge difference in your cost and the type of coverage you can get.

Your occupation and your income are two of the biggest factors that determine your rate and the type of coverage you can qualify for. The toughest jobs to cover aren't ones you'd immediately think of as risky. Doctors, dentists, the self-employed, and anyone who works from home, for an example, can have a surprisingly difficult time qualifying for good coverage.

Engineers, CPAs, attorneys, and executives generally don't have any trouble getting own-occupation coverage that pays out until age 65, if they're in good health. They usually pay a lower rate if they don't travel frequently or if their job is less risky than others in a similar occupation. A home builder in management who primarily works in the office, for example, will generally pay less than a builder who spends his time on the construction site. When applying for the policy, it helps to provide the broker with details about your job and income, so he knows up front which companies to focus on and how to present your case to the insurer.

The prices are reasonable for those types of jobs. A midlevel executive who earns about $55,000 per year and travels occasionally could buy a Berkshire Life policy with a 90-day waiting period, a $3,000 monthly benefit for life, a cost-of-living adjustment, and a few other features for about $1,930 per year if he buys the policy at age 40 or $2,850 if he buys it at age 50, says John Ryan of Ryan Insurance Strategy Consultants, a Greenwood Village, Colorado, firm that helps fee-only financial advisors with insurance. Women pay a lot more because they tend to file more claims—the same policy would cost $2,975 for a 40-year-old woman; $3,690 for a 50-year-old woman. Once they buy the policy, the price will never change. If the executive earned $130,000, he or she could get a policy with a $6,000 monthly benefit for almost double the price. The price drops a bit for top executives earning over $200,000 and traveling less frequently—from $1,929 to $1,775 per year for a man and from $2,975 to $2,740 for a woman. Lowering the benefit period from lifetime to age 65 will shave about 10 percent off the price (see Figure 7.2).

Even though many of these people can qualify for a policy that provides own-occupation coverage until age 65, they may not need it. Long-term own-occupation policies tend to be best for people in

FIGURE 7.2 The Cost of Policies

The annual premiums for a policy that pays $3,000 per month, provides lifetime own-occupation benefits, a 90-day waiting period, and a cost-of-living adjustment for a midlevel executive who earns about $55,000 per year and travels occasionally are as follows:

Age When Purchasing Policy	Annual Premium
Male, age 30	$1,250
Female, age 30	$1,975
Male, age 40	$1,930
Female, age 40	$2,975
Male, age 50	$2,850
Female, age 50	$3,690

Source: John Ryan, Ryan Insurance Strategy Consultants, Greenwood Village, Colorado

highly specialized, physical fields (like surgeons) who could be side-lined by an injury and will have a tough time finding another job that pays as much. Many salaried employees in middle management, however, can switch to another job and earn nearly as much money, and if they can't then the loss of income coverage will make up the difference. If they cannot afford to buy own-occupation coverage that pays until age 65, they can lower their rate by buying a policy that only provides own-occupation coverage for five years, then becomes a loss of income policy after that, which will buy them time to figure out what to do next. Most disability insurance claims last for much less than five years.

Dentists and doctors, especially surgeons, are some of the toughest people to insure. That's because insurers were burned in the 1990s after physicians filed record numbers of claims. They are some of the people who should consider own-occupation coverage, especially if they are in a highly specialized field and unlikely to make as much money in another job. However, they may only qualify for limited own-occupation coverage, especially if they're surgeons (see the next section).

Self-employed people can have a hard time finding coverage, especially if they have a new business and short earnings record, because it's tough to predict what their income will be. You'll have an easier time if you remain in the same line of business where you worked before and have annual contracts with clients, assuring some regular income. Otherwise, you may not be able to get a policy until you can submit a tax return from at least one year in that business. If there's any chance you'll become self-employed in the future, it's a good idea to get an individual disability policy while you still have a full-time job (although you'll usually have to do this several years before you go out on your own).

People who work in a home office have a notoriously difficult time getting coverage—even if they're just a consultant or freelance writer who sits at a computer all day. Insurers worry that it's tough to prove whether or not they're really disabled because they don't need to go anywhere. A few years ago, people who worked from home could only get a policy with a five-year benefit period and no coverage after that, but now you can get coverage to age 65 if you leave the home office 50 to 60 percent of the time to conduct business, says John Ryan. You'll have a tougher time if you don't leave your home for business, which seems less risky but makes you tougher for the insurance company to monitor.

Doctors should shop around for disability insurance again if they bought a policy a few years ago. They may be able to find much better coverage now.

Disability insurance companies spent a lot of time marketing rich benefits packages to doctors in the 1980s. They'd provide own-occupation coverage, paying full benefits for a surgeon, for example, if he had back trouble and could no longer do surgery but could earn just as much money by working for a biotech firm. With the disability payout and new job, he could essentially double his income. The policy benefit limits were high—sometimes offering $25,000 in monthly coverage, depending on the physician's income level when he applied for the policy.

The insurers suffered financially in the 1990s when an unexpected number of policyholders ended up filing claims. One reason for the spike in claims, insurers explained, was caused by managed care. Doctors whose income dropped substantially after HMOs entered their business may have been less motivated to keep working. Some discovered that they could get more money by going on claim than by continuing in their jobs—especially if they had an own-occupation policy that would pay full benefits even if they earned a lot of money somewhere else. The number of claims boomed for conditions that were tough to verify, such as back pain, fibromyalgia, chronic fatigue syndrome, and mental and nervous disorders.

Insurers ended up with big financial problems after having to pay out the record number of claims, and generally weren't allowed to raise prices for current policyholders, who had noncancelable and guaranteed renewable policies. As a result, many insurers ended up leaving the business and selling their policies to other companies, which now service the claims. Dozens of insurance companies sold individual disability coverage in the 1980s. By 2002, just ten insurers were selling 90 percent of the new policies, according to Conning Research & Consulting, an insurance-research firm.

Insurers couldn't do much about the policies they already sold— they weren't even allowed to raise rates in most cases—but because of this bad experience, many insurance companies cut back on their coverage significantly for new customers, shunning doctors, dentists, and other professionals who had a lot of claims, shrinking their benefit limits, and cutting back benefit periods. They used to pay lifetime benefits if someone couldn't do their own occupation, even if they found another job that paid just as much. After the shake-up, they only offered two years of own-occupation coverage—and none at all for some professions—and would only pay after that if the person couldn't do any occupation. They also started to cap monthly benefits at $10,000 or less, and cut benefits completely at age 65.

Since then, however, a few insurers started to loosen their standards over the past few years. Some people can now get up to $15,000 per month in coverage, although doctors and dentists are generally still limited to $10,000 in monthly payouts. Engineers, CPAs, attorneys, executives, and even some types of doctors can get own-occupation coverage until age 65. Most companies only offer surgeons own-occupation coverage for five years. After that their policies either won't pay out at all if they find another job, or will only pay the difference between their old income and their new income.

The marketplace continues to change, and a few companies, like MetLife, now offer own-occupation coverage with lifetime benefits to physicians, and the type of doctor makes a big difference. A surgeon who buys a policy with a $3,000 monthly benefit at age 40 could pay $2,400 per year; or $3,150 if he buys it at age 50 ($3,475 and $3,775 for a woman), says Ryan. A noninvasive doctor, generally a physician other than a surgeon, could pay $2,150 if he buys the policy at age 40 or $2,800 if he buys it at age 50 ($3,100 and $3,370 for a woman). (See Figure 7.3.)

FIGURE 7.3 Doctors' Cost for Coverage

A few companies now offer own-occupation coverage with lifetime benefits to physicians, after years of pulling back on this type of coverage. Here's how much a surgeon and other physician will pay for a policy that pays $3,000 per month, provides lifetime own-occupation benefits, a 90-day waiting period, and a cost-of-living adjustment, based on the age when they purchase the policy:

Doctors with Invasive Specialties (such as surgeons)

Age at Present	Annual Premiums
Male, age 30	$1,325
Female, age 30	$2,100
Male, age 40	$2,400
Female, age 40	$3,475
Male, age 50	$3,150
Female, age 50	$3,775

Doctors with Noninvasive Specialties (most nonsurgeons)

Age at Present	Annual Premiums
Male, age 30	$1,200
Female, age 30	$1,890
Male, age 40	$2,150
Female, age 40	$3,100
Male, age 50	$2,800
Female, age 50	$3,370

Source: John Ryan, Ryan Insurance Strategy Consultants, Greenwood Village, Colorado

People who were rejected in the past because of their health may be able to qualify for coverage now.

Now is a good time to shop around again for disability insurance if you were rejected or charged a high rate because of your medical condition.

A few years ago, insurers rejected almost anyone who sought help for their mental health, worrying that it could lead to a long and expensive claim for mental and nervous disorders. Now, if you're in counseling for a particular situation, such as marriage counseling or grief counseling after a death in the family, you may be able to get coverage until age 65, even if you're on medication. The insurer will generally exclude coverage for mental and nervous disorders, but would have rejected you entirely in the past.

In the past, you also had little hope of finding a policy if you had cancer, diabetes, a heart attack, or were overweight. Now you might qualify for an impaired-risk policy, which generally provides less coverage at higher prices, but at least will provide you with some coverage.These impaired-risk policies generally have a stricter definition of disability (excluding mental and nervous disorders for people with a history of those conditions, for example), the benefit period is shorter, and the insurer generally only pays a portion of the benefit amount in the early years—paying 30 to 40 percent of the full benefit amount if you become disabled in year one, for example, 60 to 70 percent in year two, and 100 percent in year three or beyond. The policies tend to cost about 25 percent more than standard coverage and the price can increase through time.

The rules vary a lot depending on the details of the condition, how well you're controlling it, and how long you've been living with the disease. With most types of coverage, you generally need to be cancer-free for at least two years before you can get coverage. A disability insurance broker should know which companies are most likely to insure people with your condition and can help present your case, often sending the insurance company a cover letter explaining how you've managed your disease and why you may be less of a risk than someone else with a similar profile would be.

Check out the insurance company's complaint record. Some have bad reputations for denying claims.

Disability insurance has gotten a lot of bad press over the past few years. UnumProvident, one of the largest disability insurance companies, was involved in several high-profile million-dollar lawsuits for unfairly denying or terminating claims. The company received a $15 million fine in 2004 after the insurance regulators in every state banded together to investigate the company's sales practices. The regulators also required the company to reevaluate 300,000 claims it denied over the past several years, and California Insurance Commissioner John Garamendi came to a separate settlement with Unum-Provident in late 2005, when the company agreed to pay an $8 million fine to the California Department of Insurance and reassess 26,000 claims for California policyholders whose claims were terminated or denied from January 1, 1997, through September 30, 2005.

Many companies have had few complaints, though. You can easily find this information by checking the company's complaint record with your state insurance department and its national complaint record at the National Association of Insurance Commissioners' Consumer Information Service database (*www.naic.org/cis*). See Chapter 3 for details about how to look up a company's complaint record.

TIPS FOR GETTING THE RIGHT DISABILITY INSURANCE COVERAGE AT THE BEST PRICE

If you'd have trouble paying your bills if you were unable to work, then you should have disability insurance. Disability insurance can be incredibly complicated to shop for because it comes with its own language that is tough to translate and each company's policy is very different. Here's how to find the right policy for you and get the best deal:

- Employer disability insurance provides a lot less coverage than most people realize—only replacing up to 60 percent of your base income, not counting commissions or bonuses, with a monthly coverage cap of $5,000 to $10,000. Taxes are then subtracted if your employer paid the premiums. If you cannot live on 60 percent of your current income, or less if your salary is higher, then an individual disability insurance policy can fill in some of those gaps.

- Tiny variations in wording can make a huge difference in coverage. You can't just compare policies based on price. Look very carefully at the policy's definition of disability, which will determine whether or not your claim gets paid. An own-occupation policy is valuable if you're in a highly specialized field. A loss of income policy can still pay some benefits if you earn less at your new job, but some policies won't pay anything if you end up with a new job that pays a lot less than your old one.

- Look for a policy that is noncancelable and guaranteed renewable, which means the insurer can't raise rates as long as you pay your premiums.

- Your occupation can make a big difference in your ability to get coverage. Doctors, dentists, people who are self-employed, and especially people that work at home will have a tougher time finding coverage. Work with a broker who knows which companies generally offer the best deals—and best type of coverage—for someone like you.

- Doctors who bought a policy in the past few years should shop around again. Insurers pulled back on coverage for these professions after paying more claims than expected in the 1990s, but now they're offering better coverage, longer own-occupation benefit periods, and higher benefit limits.

- People in poor health should shop for a policy again, too. Insurers have made it easier for people with diabetes, cancer, a heart attack, or weight issues to get coverage, even if they've been rejected in the past. You may end up with an impaired risk company, which provides less coverage at a higher price, but it can still provide some protection. You generally need to be cancer-free for at least two years to get any coverage, and it can help to send the insurer a cover letter explaining how you've been controlling your condition.
- Check out the insurance company's complaint record. A large disability insurer has been involved in several high-profile lawsuits for unfairly denying or terminating claims, and paid giant fines to state regulators. Check out your insurer's complaint record at your state insurance department and through the National Association of Insurance Commissioners database to help avoid companies with bad reputations.

INSURANCE NEEDS THROUGHOUT YOUR LIFE

■ ■ ■

Every time you make a major life change, your insurance needs change, too. Here's how to find the best deals and protect yourself and your family throughout your lives.

INSURANCE NEEDS WHEN YOU GRADUATE FROM COLLEGE

■ Find your own health insurance. You can generally stay on your parents' health insurance policy while you're a full-time student, up to age 25 (the rules vary by company). After that, you can keep that coverage for up to 36 months through COBRA, a federal law that lets you continue the coverage temporarily after you leave the group. The price, however, will jump because the employer is no longer subsidizing part of the bill. Sign up for COBRA so that you know you have some coverage, no matter what happens, then search for a better deal. If you don't have health insurance through an employer, shop for an individual policy, which can be a lot less expensive than COBRA when you're young and healthy. Consider buying a high-deductible health insurance policy and opening a health savings account, which can save you money in premiums and build long-term savings you can use tax-free for future medical expenses. Consider a short-term health insurance policy if you expect to get coverage through an employer within a few months.

- Buy renters insurance for your apartment. Your personal belongings can be surprisingly expensive to replace and it's important to have the liability coverage in case anyone gets hurt in your home. A renters policy can cost as little as $100 to $200 per year and covers your possessions as well as provides liability coverage.

- Get your own auto insurance policy. Now that you're no longer a teenager, you won't be in the most expensive group anymore (although the coverage is still pricey when you're in your early 20s). You can save a lot of money by raising your deductibles, buying a safe car, improving your credit score, and shopping around for the best deal.

- You probably don't need life insurance yet unless you're married, have children, or someone else who is depending on you financially.

INSURANCE NEEDS WHEN YOU GET MARRIED

- If you both work, each of you now has a slew of new health insurance choices. Check out all of your options—such as remaining on your own employer's policy, shifting one spouse to the other's employer's policy, or buying medical coverage through one spouse's employer while getting dental coverage through another. Some employers will give you a bonus if you forego their policy and get coverage through your spouse's company instead.

- Buy life insurance if you have a mortgage or other big bills and your spouse depends on your income. If you both work and could cover the bills on your own, you may not need life insurance yet.

- Whenever you first move in with your spouse or partner, add him or her to your homeowners or renters insurance policy and boost your property coverage to include his or her stuff. Get a separate rider for the engagement ring and other valuables worth more than $1,000.

- Combine auto insurance policies. If you have coverage with two different companies now, get price quotes for switching both cars to the same company, which will earn you a multicar discount. You may also get a price break for getting married, which some insurers think makes you a better risk.

- Calculate whether you need more disability insurance. If you have coverage through your employer, is that enough to cover your bills if you couldn't work? If not, consider getting extra coverage.

INSURANCE NEEDS WHEN YOU BUY A HOUSE

- Boost your life insurance and disability insurance amount to make sure your family has enough money to cover your mortgage payments, in addition to your other bills.

- Before you buy a house, check out its CLUE report—insurers share information about a person's and a house's claims experience in this database, and you might have a tough time getting coverage on the home if a lot of claims were filed even before you moved there.

- Shop around for homeowners insurance. Check first with your auto insurance company, which may offer you a discount for having both kinds of coverage with them. Also compare rates for other companies—the price range can be wide from company to company.

- Tell your auto insurance company about your house. Some insurers consider homeowners to be better risks, and your rates may also drop if you now park your car in a garage and move to a quieter area.

INSURANCE NEEDS WHEN YOU HAVE A BABY

- If you don't already have life insurance, this is usually the key time to buy a policy, now that someone is definitely depending on you financially. Also get coverage for stay-at-home parents, because childcare will be very expensive if anything happens to them.
- Make sure you have enough disability insurance to cover your family's bills if you become disabled and cannot work.
- Update your health insurance to cover the baby. Check out all of your coverage options through you and your spouse's employer again, because your medical needs are now a lot different than they were before the baby (many more routine doctor's visits).

INSURANCE NEEDS IF YOU GET A NEW JOB

- Because so much of your insurance ties in with your job, you'll need to reassess most of your coverage when you switch employers. Check all of your health insurance options again, both through your own and your spouse's employer.
- Calculate how much disability coverage your new employer offers. Even if you had ample coverage in the past, you may need to get a policy on your own to make up the difference now.

■ Make sure you have enough life insurance. If your new employer is offering less life insurance or your income is higher, you may need to boost your coverage amount.

■ Tell your auto insurance company about your new job. Your rates may drop if you have a shorter commute.

INSURANCE NEEDS WHEN YOUR CHILDREN GO TO COLLEGE

■ Let your auto insurance company know that your child is at college. If your child moves more than 100 miles away and doesn't take a car, your premiums could drop significantly while still providing coverage when he or she returns home for vacation. If the child takes a car to the school, the premiums may drop or rise depending on the locale.

■ Your child is generally eligible for health insurance on your policy while a full-time student, up to age 25. If your child's student status drops below full-time, you may need to switch him or her to COBRA coverage on your policy. Your child may get a better deal, however, by buying an individual policy—which may be inexpensive if he or she is young and healthy—or getting a short-term policy. Consider a high-deductible policy with a health savings account, which can keep the premiums low and let the child build a stash of money that he or she can use tax-free for future medical expenses.

■ Tell your homeowners insurance company that your child is at college. Your policy generally covers possessions in a dorm room, but the limits may be low so you might want to boost the amount to provide enough coverage for a new computer system and other expensive electronics that your child takes to school. If your child lives off-campus, consider a renters insurance policy, which can cost just $100 to $200 for coverage on their possessions and liability coverage.

INSURANCE NEEDS WHEN YOUR NEST IS EMPTY

- Call your auto insurance company after your children are on their own. Your premiums should—finally—drop significantly now that your children are off your policy.
- Your health insurance policy generally doesn't cover children when they are no longer full-time students. They can continue coverage under your employer's policy for up to 36 months under COBRA, but the price rises because the employer is no longer subsidizing part of the bill. Still, sign up for COBRA so you know there is some coverage, and then you can drop it later if they get jobs with health benefits or find better deals on their own. Consider a high-deductible policy with a health savings account or a short-term policy if your child doesn't have employee coverage. After your children are off your policy, review all of your own health insurance options again— your health insurance needs may be very different now that your children are no longer on your policy, and another one of your employer's options may be a better deal.
- Reassess your life insurance needs. Once your children are on their own, you may not need life insurance anymore or you may be able to decrease the coverage amount, depending on your other bills and your spouse's dependence on your income.
- Now that you have fewer family obligations, consider buying long-term care insurance. The younger you are when you buy it, the lower the price, but you'll pay the premiums for more years. Many people find they can afford long-term care insurance after dropping life insurance when their children are on their own.

INSURANCE NEEDS AFTER YOU RETIRE

- You may finally be able to drop your life insurance (if you haven't already)—even if your spouse is relying on you financially—as long as your spouse has pension death benefits.
- Consider buying long-term care insurance if you haven't already. It's essential to protect your retirement savings from the potentially devastating expenses.
- Tell your auto insurance company when you retire. You may get a retiree discount and your premiums may also drop if you no longer commute to work.
- Tell your homeowners insurance company when you retire. You may get a discount now that you are around the house more often during the day.
- If you have retiree health insurance, you're lucky—that's usually your best bet, even if you're paying a lot more than you did as an employee. If you retire before age 65 and don't have retiree health benefits, you can keep your coverage through COBRA for up to 18 months. You'll pay more without the employer subsidy, but this could still be your best option if you have any medical conditions. Otherwise, you may find a better deal by buying a high-deductible policy and opening a health savings account, which can build up savings you can use tax-free for medical expenses at any age. Even after you qualify for Medicare, there are still plenty of medical bills to spend the HSA money on.
- When you reach age 65, sign up for Medicare and quickly decide how you'll fill in the gaps, whether it's through a medigap policy or a Medicare Advantage plan. If you buy a policy within six months of signing up for Medicare Part B, then the insurer can't raise your rate or deny you coverage because of your medical condition. Decide whether or not you need to buy Medicare prescription drug coverage, which is generally important to get unless you already have better coverage through a former employer or other source.

One of the main reasons why so many people are intimidated and confused when shopping for insurance is because the insurance business has its own language. It's tough to ask questions or know exactly what you're buying when an agent or insurance company is overwhelming you with jargon. Here are some of the key words to help with the translation, so you know what they're talking about.

Actual cash value A method homeowners insurance companies use to value your possessions. Actual cash value assumes depreciation, in other words, how much it would cost to replace the item with another used item of its age today. Replacement value, on the other hand, pays the cost to buy the same item new today, which is generally a much better deal.

Actuary The person in an insurance company who assesses your risk and determines your rate.

Attained age The method some medigap insurers use to adjust your rates through time. With attained-age policies, your premiums increase as you get older, typically jumping every one, three, or five years (in addition to price increases due to healthcare inflation, which can happen to all medigap policies). It's generally better to look for an issue-age policy instead, where premiums are based on your age when you originally buy the policy and usually don't increase as much through time.

Cash value life insurance A life insurance policy that provides
insurance coverage and a savings account. Unlike term insurance, you can keep the policy for the rest of your life not just
20 or 30 years. There are three main types of cash value insurance: whole life, universal life, and variable universal life. The
premiums, however, tend to be a lot higher than they are for
term insurance.

CLUE report The report from the Comprehensive Loss Underwriting Exchange, the database where most auto and homeowners insurance companies share information about the previous
losses filed by a person or on a particular home. If insurers see
a lot of claims on your CLUE report (or on the report for your
home), you may have a tougher time finding affordable coverage anywhere.

COBRA The federal law that requires most companies with 20 or
more employees to let you stay on their health insurance plan
for a certain time period after you leave the group. You can
keep your group health insurance through COBRA for up to
18 months after you leave your job, or can remain on your
former spouse's employer plan for up to 36 months after you
get divorced, and your children can keep the coverage for up
to 36 months after they stop qualifying for family coverage
(generally when they're no longer a full-time student or reach
age 25). You can continue the coverage under COBRA
regardless of your health, but the price jumps because you
have to pay the entire cost yourself, with no subsidy from the
employer.

Coinsurance The share of each healthcare or prescription drug bill
that you need to pay out of your own pocket, generally based on
a percentage of the total cost. Many insurers are switching from
fixed-dollar copayments to percentage-based coinsurance to try
to encourage people to become better healthcare shoppers
because they save more money themselves if they spend less on
care.

Copayments The share of each healthcare or prescription drug bill that you need to pay out of your own pocket, generally a fixed dollar amount, such as $20 for each prescription.

Creditable coverage Prescription drug coverage, generally offered through a former employer, for people over age 65, that is considered to be at least as good as Medicare's Part D plan. If you have creditable coverage, you won't be hit with a penalty if you keep your current coverage and then switch to Medicare Part D later.

Deductibles The amount you need to pay out of your pocket before insurance kicks in. Raising your deductible on your health, auto, and homeowners insurance can cut your premiums significantly, while only raising your out-of-pocket costs if you end up having large claims.

Elimination period The waiting period before a long-term care insurance policy starts to pay out. The longer the waiting period you get, the lower your premium, but the more money you have to pay out of your own pocket first. Unlike auto and homeowners insurance deductibles, it can be very expensive to pick too long of an elimination period on a long-term care policy you could get stuck paying tens of thousands of dollars out of your own pocket before the coverage kicks in.

Future purchase options A type of inflation protection in long-term care insurance where you can increase your daily benefit amount through the years but your premiums increase, too. This is very different than policies with 5 percent compound inflation protection, which generally charge higher premiums at the beginning but automatically increase your benefit amount every year without raising your premiums. Policies with future purchase options tend to be a lot more expensive over the long term than those with 5 percent compound inflation protection because the premiums for extra coverage are based on your age when you buy them, and the price rises as you get older. As a result, increasing your coverage amount at age 75, for example, can be incredibly expensive.

Gap insurance Also called "loan/lease payoff," this is extra auto insurance to pay the difference between the amount due on your loan and the car's depreciated value (its current value as a used car), which is the most that insurers will generally pay if you total your car. If you made a low down payment and took out a long loan, the gap may be several thousand dollars in the early years.

Guaranteed issue A state law that requires insurers to provide health insurance to everyone, regardless of their medical condition. Some states also pair this with community rating rules where insurers must charge everyone the same rate, regardless of their age or health. New Jersey has guaranteed issue and community rating for its individual health insurance policies; New York has guaranteed issue and modified community rating, which lets insurers adjust costs by region. Because of these laws, health insurance tends to be a lot more expensive for young and healthy people in New York and New Jersey than it is in other states.

Health savings account (HSA) Health savings accounts were introduced in 2004, as a way to save money on health insurance and get tax breaks for medical expenses. If you buy a high-deductible health insurance policy (with deductibles, in 2006, of at least $1,050 for individuals and $2,100 for families) and meet a few other requirements, then you can set aside tax-deductible money in a health savings account up to the amount of the insurance deductible, with a maximum in 2006 of $2,700 for individuals or $5,450 for families (people age 55 or older can contribute an extra $700 in 2006). You can withdraw the money tax-free to pay for medical expenses at any age and you don't have to use the money by the end of the year. You'll owe a 10 percent penalty if you use the money for nonmedical expenses before age 65. The penalty is waived after age 65, but you'll still owe income taxes on your earnings for non-medical expenses. Most HSA administrators offer fixed-interest accounts, although more are starting to let you invest your money in mutual funds.

High-risk pool Thirty-three states have high-risk health insurance pools, which provide coverage to everyone regardless of their medical condition. They must usually be rejected by a few private insurers before they can get coverage through the pool. The pools tend to provide less coverage and charge higher prices than private insurance companies do, although most states limit the premiums the pools can charge to 125 percent or 150 percent higher than standard coverage.

Impaired risk A person who is considered a high risk by an insurance company, whether it's someone buying life insurance with a history of medical problems or a driver who has a lot of speeding tickets and accidents.

Inflation protection Long-term care and disability insurance policies that increase the benefit amount for inflation. Many long-term care insurance policies provide 5 percent compound inflation protection, which means that your benefit amount is increased by 5 percent every year but your premiums remain the same. Another way to increase your benefits through time is through future purchase options, where your premiums are lower in the beginning but you have to pay extra whenever you increase the coverage amount. In that case, the cost of the extra coverage is based on your age when you increase the benefit amount. Because the price rises a lot as you get older, the 5 percent compound inflation protection tends to be less expensive over the long run.

Issue age The method some medigap insurers use to set their rates. Issue-age policies base the price on your age when you buy the policy. If you buy it at age 65, for example, it's less expensive than if you buy it at age 70, but your premiums won't increase just because you get older (although they can rise because of healthcare inflation). These are generally a better deal than attained-age policies, because prices usually increase a lot less through time.

Mortality tables The life expectancy tables that insurance companies use to estimate how long you'll live when they price their life insurance policies.

No-load policies Life insurance policies where the salesperson doesn't earn a commission. They usually have some sales and marketing charges, but tend to be much lower than those in commissioned policies, and generally have little or no surrender charges.

Noncancelable and guaranteed renewable With this type of disability insurance policy, rates cannot rise through time and the insurer cannot drop you as long as you continue to pay your premiums.

Nonowner coverage An auto insurance policy for people who don't own a car but need coverage if they rent or borrow someone else's car. It also provides you with continuous coverage, which can help qualify you for regular insurance again if you buy a car in the future. Otherwise, insurers get worried if you go for a while without auto insurance even if it's for a good reason, such as an extended trip abroad and may charge you more than someone who has had insurance all along.

Own-occupation policy A disability insurance policy that pays out if you become disabled and unable to do your job, even if you can earn more money doing another job. An own-occupation policy (also called "own-occ") would pay out in full, for example, if a surgeon hurts himself and can no longer do surgery but can earn just as much money in a new job as a medical consultant to a biotech firm. Because insurers ended up paying a lot of expensive claims in the 1990s, many now offer "modified own-occupation coverage," which only provides own-occupation coverage for the first two or three years paying in full even if you earn more money in a new job at first then dropping back after a few years and only paying out if you earn less money in your new job than you did in your old one.

Part D The new Medicare prescription drug plan. Coverage is provided by private insurance companies but approved by the government program. It is important to sign up for Part D if you don't already have better coverage through a former employer or other source.

Physical damage coverage Includes both collision, which covers damages to your own car from accidents, and comprehensive, which covers damages to your car not caused by a collision with another car (if you hit a deer or a tree falls on your car, for example).

Policy illustration The paperwork that insurers provide when you buy a cash value life insurance policy, which shows how much money the savings portion of your policy should grow to under various assumptions. With variable universal life insurance policies, for example, the illustrations generally show how the investments will grow over 20 or 30 years if the investments return 0 percent, 6 percent, or 12 percent per year. After you've had the policy for several years, ask for an "in-force illustration," which shows how well the policy is now expected to perform in the future, based on how well it has done so far (which may be a lot different from your original illustration, based on market performance).

Rate class The price category the insurance company includes you in, based on various risk factors. Each company generally has five or more rate classes for term life insurance, for example, including super-preferred (the healthiest and least expensive), preferred, standard, smoker, and various impaired-risk classes (the highest risks and most expensive).

Rider Additional coverage added to your policy. You can generally add a rider on to your homeowners insurance policy to cover your jewelry and other valuables, your home office, computer equipment, or other items that may need more insurance than the standard policy provides.

Surrender charge The penalty you pay if you drop a cash value life insurance policy in the first several years. It generally starts out at about 7 percent of your cash value within the first seven to ten years, and then gradually shrinks by 1 percent per year until it disappears entirely. These charges generally apply to policies sold by commissioned agents (to recoup commissions and sales charges). Most no-load policies do not have a surrender charge.

Term insurance Provides life insurance for a fixed time period, such as 20 or 30 years. The policy pays out the death benefit if you die during that time period, but generally pays nothing if you're still alive at the end of the term. Popular with families who have young children and only need the insurance for a certain time period. The premiums are a lot lower than they are for cash value insurance, which includes life insurance and a savings account.

Umbrella policy Also called "excess liability coverage," which covers damages and legal fees above the liability limit included in your homeowners or auto insurance policy. You must generally keep the maximum liability coverage on your homeowners or auto policy first about $500,000 or $1 million and then can get an umbrella policy to cover $1 million or several million of liability above that.

Underwriting criteria The rules the insurers set for qualifying for a policy or a particular price. In order to qualify for preferred life insurance rates, for example, your cholesterol level, blood pressure, and height/weight must generally fall within certain levels and you cannot have a history of certain medical conditions.

Universal life insurance A cash value life insurance policy where you can adjust the amount you pay into it within a certain range paying a lower premium if you primarily want life insurance or a higher premium if you want to build up more money in the savings account. The insurance company invests the money for you in bond-like investments.

Variable universal life insurance A cash value life insurance policy with the premium flexibility of universal life, but the money is invested in mutual fund-like accounts you choose from a handful of options.

Whole life insurance The original type of cash value policy, with fixed premiums for the rest of your life. The insurance company invests the money and provides dividends to increase your cash value. The premiums never change, regardless of the insurer's investment returns.

It is much easier to shop for insurance than it was a decade ago, primarily because so many Internet resources can help people with their search.

Instead of relying solely on the word of an agent, who may or may not have your best interests in mind, you can now do plenty of research on your own. Here are some of the best resources for understanding the policies, calculating your insurance needs, checking out a company, and shopping for the best deals.

HEALTH INSURANCE

- *eHealthInsurance* (*www.ehealthinsurance.com*). A great source for health insurance price quotes if you're shopping for coverage on your own. It quickly lists a variety of plans, companies, and coverage amounts, and makes it easy to see how changing the deductible and other variables can affect your price. In addition to standard health insurance, it's also a good source of information about HSA-eligible and short-term policies.
- *HSA Insider* (*www.hsainsider.com*). This is an excellent source for information about health savings accounts, including lists of companies offering the insurance plans and financial institutions providing the savings accounts.
- *HSA Finder* (*www.hsafinder.com*).You will find a great source of information about HSAs on this Web site, especially for

details about the financial institutions offering the savings accounts.

- *HealthDecisions.org* (*www.healthdecisions.org*). A list of companies providing health insurance in your state, including contact information and links to some price quotes.
- *National Association of Health Underwriters* (*www. nahu.org*). This site, run by the trade association for health insurance agents, is the best way to find a health insurance agent in your area.
- *Kaiser Family Foundation* (*www.kff.org*). This is an excellent resource for health insurance studies and statistics, especially about employer coverage.
- *Self-Employed Country's risk pool resources* (*www.selfemployedcountry.org/riskpools.html*). Communicating for Agriculture and the Self-Employed, an organization that started as a nonprofit rural advocacy group in Minnesota, now offers one of the best resources for information about state high-risk health insurance pools.
- *National Association of State Comprehensive Health Insurance Plans* (*www.naschip.org*). This is the trade group for the high-risk health insurance pools. Its Web site includes information about the pools and links to each state pool's Web site.

HEALTH INSURANCE FOR RETIREES

- *Medicare.gov* (*www.medicare.gov*). The government's site for Medicare information, which includes the best calculator for selecting a Part D prescription drug plan, finding out how much each company charges for medigap and Medicare HMOs in your state, and detailed information about how Medicare works and what it covers.

- *Medicare Rights Center* (*www.medicarerights.org*). An excellent resource for information about dealing with Medicare, strategies for finding the best medigap policy and prescription drug plan, and frequently asked questions about how the government program works.
- *AARP's Medicare Information* (*www.aarp.org/health/medicare*). Timely information about the Medicare program, picking the best coverage, and links to other helpful resources.
- *BenefitsCheckupRX* (*www.benefitscheckup.com*). An excellent tool for finding federal, state, and private programs to help pay for your prescription medications.
- *Social Security prescription drug costs help* (*www.socialsecurity .gov/prescription help*). Information and an application to apply for the low-income subsidy to help pay for Medicare's prescription drug plan, as well as links to other good resources.
- *Health Assistance Partnership program locator* (*www. healthassistancepartnership.org/program-locator/*). Links to state programs helping with all kinds of health insurance, especially to the State Health Insurance Assistance Programs (SHIP), which provide counselors to help seniors with their health insurance issues in every state.

HOMEOWNERS AND AUTO INSURANCE

- *Independent Insurance Agents and Brokers of America* (*www.iiaba.org*). The best way to find an independent insurance agent in your area. Most members specialize in auto and homeowners insurance, and many sell small-business and other types of coverage, too. Also check out the association's Trusted Choice (*www.iiaba.net/tc*) Web site to search for an agent in your area or for additional information.

- *InsWeb* (*www.insweb.com*). An insurance marketplace that provides price quotes for auto, homeowners, and other kinds of insurance from many companies. Also includes information about each kind of insurance and calculators to help you determine whether you have enough coverage.
- *ChoiceTrust* (*www.choicetrust.com*). The site where you can get a copy of your CLUE report, the information in the claims database that insurance companies share with each other about your house and your car when setting your prices. You can also order a copy of your Home and Auto Insurance Scores, a version of your credit score that homeowners and auto insurance companies use when determining your rates.
- *AccuCoverage* (*www.accucoverage.com*). The consumer site of Marshall & Swift/Boeckh, a firm that provides building-cost estimates to insurance companies, where you can find information on replacement cost and calculate whether you have enough insurance on your home.
- *Floodsmart.gov* (*www.floodsmart.gov*). The National Flood Insurance Program's Web site, where you can assess the likelihood that your property will be flooded, get price quotes for flood insurance, and find contact information for agents in your area who sell the government's flood plan.
- *MyFico* (*www.myfico.com*). The consumer site of Fair Isaac, which created the FICO credit score most lenders use. Even though your insurance score is calculated a bit differently, the advice at MyFico can help you improve both types of scores. Also check your credit record at *AnnualCreditReport.com* (*www.annualcreditreport.com*), where you can get a free copy of your credit report from each of the three bureaus once every 12 months. Because your credit score and insurance score are based on the information in your credit reports, it's important to check them frequently for errors. The site also includes links to the three credit bureaus, where you can get more information about your score and contest any errors.

- *Kelley Blue Book* (*www.kbb.com*). An excellent source for used car values, which is helpful to check when deciding whether your car's value has fallen enough that you no longer need comprehensive or collision coverage. If you take out a long car loan and make a low down payment, also check the site to see if it's worthwhile to buy gap coverage to make up the difference if the amount of money you owe on your car is more than its current depreciated value, which is the most the insurer will generally pay out if the car is totaled.

- *CarSafety.org* (*www.carsafety.org*). The Web site for the Insurance Institute for Highway Safety, which includes detailed car-safety information and crash test ratings for all cars. It also lists the safest cars in several categories.

- *The National Insurance Crime Bureau* (*www.nicb.org*). Lists the most stolen vehicles in the United States every year, which affects your auto insurance rates. Also includes information about insurance fraud and scams. After Hurricane Katrina, it provided a database of vehicle identification numbers for cars that were affected by the hurricanes, gathered from insurance companies and regulators, to help people avoid buying cars with undisclosed flood damage.

LIFE INSURANCE

- *Insure.com* (*www.insure.com*). One of the best sites for life insurance quotes. Lets you search for prices immediately and anonymously from many insurance companies, and makes it easy to see how rates compare for various terms and types of coverage. The only site to list the insurance companies' underwriting criteria for each policy, which are the details about your health, hobbies, and other information that the insurers require to qualify for each rate (such as cholesterol, blood pressure, and height/weight cut-offs).

- *AccuQuote* (*www.accuquote.com*). An excellent site for life insurance quotes. It asks for enough medical, family, and hobby information to match you up with accurate quotes from many insurance companies, and is a great source to call for help in finding the best deal if you have any medical conditions. Includes good life insurance information and calculators.
- *InsWeb* (*www.insweb.com*). Another good site for life insurance price quotes from several companies.
- *Medical Information Bureau* (*www.mib.com*). The company that keeps the medical information that life insurance companies share about you. You can get more information about the reports and order a copy of yours at their site. Also offers a service to help people track down lost life insurance policies.
- *Consumer Federation of America* (*www.consumerfed.org*). This consumer advocacy group frequently publishes studies about all types of insurance. Its life insurance evaluation service (*www.evaluatelifeinsurance.org*) is one of the best ways to determine whether it's still worthwhile to keep a cash-value policy that you've had for a while.

LONG-TERM CARE INSURANCE

- *MetLife Mature Market Institute* (*www.maturemarketinstitute.com*). The company's information and policy resource center compiles some of the best information about the average costs of nursing homes and home healthcare throughout the country. The site also includes many interesting studies and consumer resources.
- *Weiss Ratings* (*www.weissratings.com*). The insurance ratings and research organization's "Consumer Guide to Long-Term Care Insurance" includes detailed information about how the

policies work, coverage you may and may not need, and sample prices for various types of policies.

- *ElderWeb* (*www.elderweb.com*). A great site for resources about long-term care, care-giving, elder law, and other issues affecting seniors and their families.
- *National Academy of Elder Law Attorneys* (*www.naela.org*). A good way to search for an attorney specializing in elder-law issues, including the rules for qualifying for Medicaid and other assistance.

ALL TYPES OF INSURANCE

- *Insurance Information Institute* (*www.iii.org*). The best source of information for all kinds of insurance, with details about how each type of coverage works, frequently asked questions, timely news updates, detailed reports on insurance issues, and strategies for getting the best coverage.
- *National Association of Insurance Commissioners* (*www.naic .org*). The association of state insurance regulators Web site includes inside information, reports about the insurance business, and consumer alerts. Its Consumer Information Source (*www.naic.org/cis*) is an excellent resource for looking up an insurance company's complaint history.
- *Kiplinger.com* (*www.kiplinger.com*). Provides information and advice about all kinds of personal finance and insurance issues, including links to state regulators and calculators to help you determine your insurance needs.
- *Weiss Ratings* (*www.weissratings.com*). Resource for insurance company financial-strength ratings, consumer guides for buying Medicare supplement, long-term care, and other types of insurance, and detailed information about the insurance business.

■ *State insurance department Web sites.* The state insurance regulators' Web sites are an excellent source of information about finding an insurance company in your area, looking up its complaint history, and any other problems, and for dealing with state insurance laws. The sites generally include premium information for each type of insurance, consumer guides to help you find the best coverage, and details about how to complain if you have a problem with your insurance company. See the NAIC's Web site (*www.naic.org/state_web_map.htm*) or the insurance page at Kiplinger's Web site (*www.kiplinger.com/personalfinance/money/insurance*) for links to each state regulator's site.

■ *Insurance company Web sites.* Most insurance company sites are now filled with a ton of helpful information, including details about their policies, discounts, price quotes, information about each type of coverage, and insurance-needs calculators.